88 C Programs

by JT Kalnay

88 C Programs

This book is dedicated to Dennis Ritchie and to Steve Jobs.

To Dennis for giving us the tools to program.

To Steve for giving us a reason to program.

About This Book

This book is not organized in a traditional chapter format.

Instead I have chosen to include example programs that exhaustively illustrate the important points of C in an evolutionary manner. By working through these programs you can teach yourself C. I assume you already know how to program and are familiar with standard algorithms.

The programs that I present are not, by themselves, complete applications. The programs are "single-issue teaching programs". Experienced programmers who are learning a new language have told me time and time again that they mainly want to see the functionality of the new syntactic and semantic elements. The programmers tell me that they will be able to think of the applicability of the feature to their project. When necessary, I provide a sample application to give a feel for how the new element might be employed.

The programs are presented in an order that presents the simplest, most straightforward aspect of a new element first. Subsequent programs present the more subtle or confusing aspects of a new element. This is a proven pedagogical approach for teaching C that I have presented to over 1,000 professionals and college students.

This book assumes that you are already a programmer and are able to learn well on your own.

Good luck in your study of C.

Table Of Contents

Simple.c   simplest C program, main, program entry point

helloworld.c   one printf

prog1.c   more printf

prog2.c   comments, case sensitivity

prog3.c   variable declaration and initialization

prog4.c   printf output

ops.c   C operators

prog4a.c   printf output

prog5.c   C data types

pg34.c   sizeof(var)

prog6.c   operators and precedence

prog7.c   mixed mode arithmetic

prog8.c   modulus

steve.c   relational operators

prog9a.c   three types of loops

prog10.c   for loop

prog11.c   for loop, scanf

prog12.c   nested for loops

prog13.c   while loop

prog14.c   while loop

prog15.c	while loop, do loop
if.c	if statements
16.c	math.h
19.c	logical operators and expressions
20.c	complex decision structures
21.c	switch statement
errors.c	common syntax errors
22.c	arrays
23.c	array boundaries
25.c	more array boundaries
26.c	bowling scores, arrays
27.c	character arrays
29.c	function declaration and usage
30.c	calling subroutines
31.c	passing constants to subroutines
32.c	passing variables to subroutines
33.c	subroutine returning value
35.c	multiple files compiled together
valref.c	call by reference, call by value
36.c	passing array to subroutines
37.c	passing pointer to subroutine
38.c	sorting array of integers

sortstep.c	sorting example
39.c	two dimensional array
twodim.c	two dimensional array to subroutine
testarrays.c	more arrays
testarrays1.c	more arrays
prog40.c	static, automatic, global
scope.c	scope of variables
41.c	recursion
testpop.c	stack
42.c	struct keyword, structures
43.c	structures
45.c	UNIX time.h file
46.c	Arrays of Structures
47.c	structures and arrays
48.c	strlen string processing
49.c	strcat
50.c	strcmp
52.c	getchar gets
53.c	ctype.h, string functions
charlarge.c	characters as large integers
55.c	structures and strings
57.c	pointers

58.c	pointers
59.c	pointers to structures
60.c	linked list pointers
	malloc, memory allocation
valref.c	pointers and functions
76.c	getchar, putchar
77.c	file operations, fopen, fprintf, fclose, getc, putc
uitp.c	file i/o and string processing
argtest.c	arc, argv, dealing with command line arguments
envtest.c	interface to UNIX environment
sol20.c	argc, argv
78.c	register const storage qualifiers
speed1.c	inefficiency
speed2.c	efficiency
64.c	copying strings using pointers
73.c	printf in depth
74.c	scanf in depth
75.c	scanf in depth
67.c	bit operations
bits.c	int octal hex binary display
71.c	#ifdef conditional compile
quicksort.c	quicksort pointer example
ptrtofunc.c	pointers to functions

Simple.c   Simplest C program possible

```
main ( )

{

}
```

main is a C keyword.

It is the program entry point.

It does not need to be in column one.

main may take arguments. We will deal with them later.

The empty round brackets ( ) indicate that we aren't going to worry about the argument list at this point.

A C comment is enclosed by /* ……. */

```
main ( )   /* program entry point */
{        /* start of block, start of scope */

        Block body

        Block blody

        …

        Block body

}        /* end of block */
```

{ is the start of scope character

} is the end of scope character

{ and } are referred to as "curly brackets" in this text.

See also "simplest C program possible: Part II full ANSI! compatability" on page 20.2

hello_world.c   Simple program with printf output

All C statements end with a semicolon   ;

```c
main ( )
{
        /* printf is a c subroutine that you get access to through the standard io library */

        /* we will cover #include <stdio.h> later */


        /* in its simplest form printf takes a character string to display */

        /* it may also take other arguments, we will examine these later */
        /* printf returns a count of the number of characters it displayed */

        /* the count can be ignored */
        printf("hello world \n");

}
```

prog1.c   More on Printf

```c
/* stdio.h is the standard input library that provides printf, scanf, and other i/o routines */

/* #include tells the compiler where to look for input/output routines you call */

/* #include < name of .h file >  will add that .h file to your compilation module */

#include <stdio.h>

int main ( )

{

        /* curly brackets mark the beginning and end of the scope of a compound statement.

        A compound statement may be a function body, the body of a loop, the body of a
        conditional,

         several statements, …   */

        printf("C Programming\n");

        printf("C Programming\n");

}

  printf("string to display"); /* string to display is inside quotations" */

  /* can provide format specifiers that describe HOW to display things (e.g., as integers, as strings) */

  /* if you put in a format specifier you need to provide a variable to satisfy the format specifier */

  printf("string format specifier", variables to satisfy format specifiers);
```

progl.c supplemental variable declaration, printf output, return value

/* to compile with ansi compiler with defaults

      acc prog1.c will produce a.out

      if (ompile is successful no "success indicator" is generated

      if errors, compiler messages will be generated

      executable can be run by typing a.out */

/* to compile with ansi compiler and specify executable's name

      acc -o   progl prog1.c

      will produce progl if (ompile is
      successful */

/* to pass source code through a very picky pre compiler

      alint progr1.c

*/

/* curly brackets mark the beginning and end of the scope of a compound statement.

      A compound statement may be a function body, the body of
      a loop, the body of a conditional, several statements */

 /* c is an expression language

      every statement returns a value,

      which may be discarded or ignored if unneeded */

/* the next program shows that printf returns the number of characters it printed. */

C Programming

value of xyz is 14

C Programming


```c
#include <stdio.h>
int main()

{

        /* int declares xyz as a variable of type integer */

        int xyz;


        /* xyz gets return value from printf */

        xyz = printf("C Programming\n");


        /* %i format specifier says print out the value of xyz as an integer */



        printf("value of xyz is %i \n",xyz);


        /* we can ignore the return value of printf */

        /* \n is the newline character */



        printf("C Programming\n");

        } /* program exit point */
```

Compile, link, run sequence

You can compile C modules to produce object files

You can assemble Assembler modules to produce object files

You can also compile other (e.g., Fortran, Pascal) programs to produce object files

You can then link all these together

ACC stands for ANSI C compiler

Acc name_of_c_file produces executable a.out

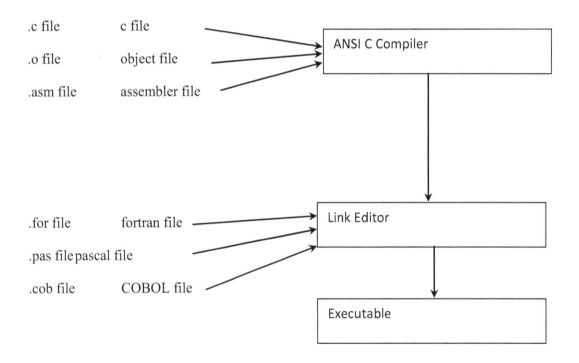

.c file   c file

.o file   object file

.asm file   assembler file

ANSI C Compiler

.for file   fortran file

.pas file pascal file

.cob file   COBOL file

Link Editor

Executable

prog2.c   comments case sensitivity

```
#include <stdio.h>

int
main ( )
{
/* comments start with slash asterisk

        can span several lines, and end with asterisk slash */

        int foobar;    /* variable names are case sensitive */

        /* all C statements except comments are case sensitive

            int is OK,  INT is not */

        /* white space is ignored */

        printf("C Programming\n");
        printf("For fun and profit\n");   /* comments can be at the end of a line */


        printf ("Hello /* this is not a comment */ dolly \n");
        print/*comment cannot be nested*/f("H1\n");        ←——— Compiler Error


        printf("abc\n");                /* comments that span lines
        printf("det\n");                can cause unexpected results... */

        /* the printf("det \n"); statement would not be compiled b/c it is inside a comment!
*/
                                                            Compiler Error
        Printf("value of foobar is %i\n",Foobar);    ←————

}
```

15

Storage Classes

Table I

Type	How Declared	Where Stored	Initial Value	Scope	Lifetime
Auto	Auto keyword or in function or in block	Stack	None	Function or block	Function or block
Static internal	Static keyword in function or block	Heap	Zero if not explicitly initialized	Function or block	Entire life of program
External	Outside all functions	Heap	Zero if not explicitly initialized	Entire program	Entire life of program
Register	Register keyword	A register, if one is available	None	Same as auto	Same as auto
Static external	Static keyword outside all functions	Heap	Zero if not explicitly initialized	Same file after definition	Entire life of program

C supports different storage classes that you can force by using explicit keywords.

prog3.c variable declaration and initialization

```c
#include <stdio.h>

int main( )
{

    /* declare an integer */
    int x;

    /* do not count on uninitialized variables to have a certain value */

    /* they could be zero and probably will be zero but, could be ??? */
        printf("Unitialized x = %i\n",x);

    x = 1 + 2;

    printf("x with 1 + 2 = %i\n", x);

}
```

Different ways to declare and initialize variables

Type_of_variable	name_of_variable
Int	x;
Float	y;
Char	c;

type_of_ variable	name1, name2, … ;
int	x,y,z;
float	f1 ,f2;
char	c1, /* first char * /
	c2; /* another char * /

type_of_ variable	name_of_ variable =	initial_value;
int	a	= 7;
float	f1	= 6.7f;

type name = initial, name = initial, ... ;
int a = 6, b = 13, c = 12;

prog4.c   printf output of variables

```c
#include <stdio.h>

/* this program adds two integer values and */

/* displays the results */

/* it also demonstrates two ways to initialize a variable */

int main( )
{
        /* declare variables */

        int v l; int v2; int vsum;

        /* declare and initialize variable */

        int all_in_one = 5;

        /* initialize values */

        v l = 1;

        v2 = 2;

        /* compute */

        vsum = v l + v2;

        /* print result */
        printf("The sum of %i and %i is %i\n",vI,v2,vsum);

        /* display all in one */
        printf("all_in_one => %i \n",all_in_one);

        /* case sensitivity error, would not compile */

        /* printf("all_in_one => %i \n",ALL_in_one);  */

        /* printf error * /

        print("all_in_one => %i \n",all_in_one);

}
```

OPERATORS: RETURN VALUE AND SIDE EFFECTS

In C, all operators have a return value and some have "side effects"

A return value isa value given back. For example in the code:

int a;

8= 3 + 4;

The addition operator (+) returns the result of adding the values 3 and 4.

A side effect is a change in a memory location. For example:

int a;

a= 7;

The assignment operator (=) changes the memory location we call 'a' to contain the value 7.

The assignment operator also has a return value, namely the new value of a (in our case 7). In this way we can say:

int a,b,c;

a=b=c=7;

7 is assigned into c, c's new value (7) is assigned into b, etc.

NOTE: any statement that has no side effecvt and who's return value is not used adds zero value

to a program.

3 + 4;

the 3 and 4 are added returning 7 which is discarded (like all intermediate results when no longer

needed). Most compilers would flag a line like 3 + 4; with the warning:

"Statement has no effect"

mathematics operators

addition   +

subtraction   -

multiplication *

division   /

assignment   =

incrementing ++

decrementing --

ops.c   program to demonstrate c operators

```
main ( )
{
        int i.x:
        i = 0;
        x = i++;        /* post increment, return vaule is OLD value, side effect is
increment*/
        printf("i = %i x = %i \n",i ,x);
        i =0;
        x = ++i;        /* pre increment, return vaule is NEW value, side effect is
increment*/
        printf("i = %i x = %i \n", i, x);
        i = 0;
        x = i--;        /* post decrement, return vaule is OLD value, side effect is
decrement*/
        printf("i = %i x = %i \n", i, x);
        i = 0;
        x = --i;        /* pre decrement, return vaule is NEW value, side effect is decrement
*/
        printf("i = %i x = %i \n", i, x);
        /* compound assignments: var op= value is the same as var = val op value
```

```
        */
        i = 5;
        i += 2;            /* plus equals, add and assign, same as i = i + 2 */
        printf("i = %i \n",i);
        i = 5;
        i -= 3;            /*  minus equals same as i = i - 3*/
        printf("i = %i \n",i);
        i = 5;
        i *= 4;            /* times equals same as i = i * 4 */
        printf("i = %i \n",i);
        i = 20;
        i /= 2;            /* divides equals same as i = i /2 */
        printf("i = %i \n",i);
        i = 25;
        i %= 7;            /* mod equals same as i = i %
7*/
        printf("i = %i \n",i);
}
```

Sample Output From ops.c

```
i= 1 x = O
i=1  x =  1
i= -1 x= O
i= -1 x= -1
i = 7
i = 2
i = 20
i = 10
i = 4
```

Exercise 1

/* make a file named xone.c */

/* write a C program to compute the following */

/* the result of b squared - 4 times a times c */

/* where a is 5, b is 4, c is 3 */

/* print out the answer * /

/* use variables named a, band c and a variable to hold the result */

/* C does not have a built in square function

nor does it have a "to the power of" operator*/

Solution for Exercise 1

```c
#include <stdio.h>

int main ( )
{
        int a, b, c, result;
        a = 5;
        b = 4;
        c = 3;
        result = ( b * b) – (4 * a * c);
        /* using the ( ) removes doubts about the order of operations... */

        printf("%i squared - ( 4 * %i * %i ) => %i \n", b,a,c,result);


}
```

Exercise 2

/* fix this program by typing it in from scratch

find the syntax errors and fix them as you go (let the compiler find the errors)

until it compiles cleanly and runs cleanly and produces the answer 12 */

```
#include stdio.h
main
        integer i;
          do some math * /
          i=1+2+3
          /* do some more math
          i = i + i;


          print(i = %m \n, i);
}
/* desired output */
/*
i = 6              inaccurate documentation !!
*/
```

```c
#include <stdio.h>
main( )
{
        int i;

        /* do some math * /
        i  = 1 + 2 + 3;

        /* do some more math * /
        i = i + i;

        printf("i = %i \n", i);
}
/* desired output * /
/*
        i = 12
*/
```

Precompiler:

The precompiler (sometimes called Preprocessor) is the first step in the compilation process. Its purpose is to:

1) remove comments before 'real' compilation

2) perform precompiler statements (a-k-a Preprocessor directives)

Precompiler statements start with a # as the first non white space character on the line. We have already seen one:

#include <stdio.h>

This statement asks the precompiler to embed the file stdio.h into our C file at the place where the directive appears.

There are several more that we will examine:

define   perform text subtitution

#if <stmt>   conditional include of code

#ifdef <stmt>   perform text substitution

#ifndef <stmt>   if not defined, include the following code

#else   else for any #if

#elseif <stmt>   else if for any #if

#endif   end of #if block

prog4a.c   #ifdef precompiler

```
main ( )
{
        #ifdef AAA
        printf("hello from aaa\n");
#endif
#ifdef BBB
        printf("hello from bbb\n");
#else
        printf("What you don't like bbb?\n");
#endif
#ifndef CCC
        printf("defineCCC to stop me before I print again!! \n");
#endif
}
```

If you compile like this: acc prog4a.c

and run a.out, you see:

What you don't like bbb?

define CCC to stop me before I print again!!!

If you compile like this: acc -DAAA prog4a.c

and run a.out, you see:

hello from aaa

What you don't like bbb?

define CCC to stop me before I print again!!!

If you compile like this: acc -DAAA -DBBB prog4a.c

and run a.out, you will see

hello from aaa

hello from bbb

define CCC to stop me before I print again!!!

If you compile like this: acc -DCCC prog4a.c

and run a.out, you will see

What you don't like bbb?

prog5.c　　C basic data types

```
/* acc prog5.c -DCASE1 -o prog5 */
/* acc prog5.c -DCASE2 -o prog5 */
main ( )
{ /* all scalar-variables may be initialized when defined */
        /* program to show declaring variables */
        /* and initializing variables */
#ifdef CASE 1
        char    c    =    'a';
        double d     =    1.23e+45
        float   f    =    123.45;
        int     i    =    321;
  #endif

        /* EXERCISE, change these to valid values */
#ifdef CASE2
        double d = 'd';
        float f = 2;
        int i  = 1.23;
        char c = d;
  #endif
        /* display character as character */
        printf("c = %c \n",c);
        /* display character as integer */
        printf("c = %d \n\n",c);
        /* display double in scientific */
        printf("d = %e \n",d);
        /* display double in float or scientific */
        /* lets computer decide */
        printf("d = %g \n\n",d);
        /* display float as floating point */
        printf("f = %f\n\n",f);
        /* display integer as base ten integer */
        printf("i = %i \n",i);
```

30

```c
/* display integer as base 16 integer */
printf("i = %x \n\n",i);
}
```

Fundamental Data Types

To Store A Character
In C a char is just a subtype (skinny) integer. What we normally think of as a character (displayable) is simply the output to the screen from some display function. Something like 'A' is an integer in C whose value is 65 (ASCII code for A). A statement like: printf("%c", 'A');
asks C to display the character whose code is 65.

To Store Integers
char (usualy 1 byte,
8 bits)
short int (at least 2
bytes)
int (usualy the same size as a machine
word)
long int (usualy at least 4 bytes perhaps
bigger)

To Store Floating Point Numbers
float (at least 4 bytes, 7 significant
digits)
double (at least 8 bytes, 15 significant digits, may be
larger)
long double (at least 8 bytes, some compilers support 16
bytes)

To Store Unsigned Integers, Logical Values and Bit Arrays
unsigned char
unsigned short int
unsigned int
unsigned long int

To Store Explicitly Signed Ints
signed char
signed short int
signed int
signed long int
If the keyword int is removed, say from signed int, the default data type is int so the statements
signed int and signed are syntactally equivalent

built in operator sizeof(x)
  sizeof(type) returns # of bytes in that type
  sizeof(variable) returns number of bytes in that
  variable

Relationships Between Sizes of Variables

1 = sizeof(char) <= sizeof(short) <= sizeof(int) <=
sizeof(long)
sizeof(float) <= sizeof(double) <= sizeof(long double)
sizeof(char,short,int,long) = sizeof(rsigned) char,short,int,long) = sizeof(Iunsigned)
c,s,i,l)

NOTE: The following items were intentionally left to the discretion of the compiler writer:

1) whether the default is signed or unsigned if the programmer does not specify it for (har, short, int or long

2) the exact number of bytes in any data type although minimum ranges have been specified

pg34.c, illustrates sizeof(var)

NOTE: sizes of different types may vary from system to system

```
main ( )
{
        char cl; int il; short sl; unsigned ul;
        long int 11;
        printf("Size of character is %d \n",sizeof(cl)
        );
        printf("Size of short int is %d \n",sizeof(sl) );
        printf("Size of unsigned int is %d
        \n",sizeof(ul) );
        printf("Size of int is %d \n",sizeof(il) );
        printf("Size of long int is %d \n",sizeof(ll) );
}
/* sample
output */
/*
Size of character
is 1
Size of short int
is 2
Size of unsigned
int is 4
Size of     int is 4
Size of long int
```

```
is 4

*/

/* exercise:

        modify this program to find out how many bytes a float and a double consume

*

/
```

PORTABILITY CONCERNS

This is not a bad time to say a few introductory words on the issue of portability. One of the strongest arguments for making the change to the C language is that of portability. If a program is coded to the ANSI standard, it *should be* -100% portable if the target platform has

an ANSI compliant C compiler available. However, there have been many groups that have learned the hard way that they need to understand, the ANSI standard in order for their programs to work correctly cross-platform.

It is extremely important to note the following in light of our discussion of data

types:

a short integer will be at least 2 bytes, but may or may not be 4

an int will typically be the same size as a machine word, but will be at least 2 bytes

a long int will be at least 4 bytes, but could be longer

Any program that needs to be portable (and still function correctly) should be careful to use these data types correctly. Back in '93 a client/server software group learned this the hard way. Their program, which ran fine on an IBM mainframe, hung their PC (DOS machines) even though it had compiled without error or warning. Their program was riddled with counters of type int (keeping track of the number of records read etc.), which would keep track of counts sometimes reaching 1 million or more. Their mainframe compiler had 4 byte ints, their PC compiler had 2 byte ints.

(RANGE: 2 bytes = 0 to 65535 4 bytes = 0 to 4,294,967,764)

Suggestion: analyze your data first and ...

-if you mean to store 2 byte quantities use a short

-if you mean to store 4 byte quantities use a long

-if you need a data value the size of a machine word (and adjusts cross-platform)

use an int (handy when writing operating system code or interrupt handlers)

-analysis of the data will also help you decide whether you need specify signed or

unsigned, if there is a need to specify it please do so.

One last word for now ...

Many C compilers come with extra libraries supporting sound, fancy graphics, low-level hard-

ware I/O, etc. Please note that these 'add-in' libraries are generally not ANSI standard and are not supplied with many compilers. (does mouse control mean anything on a 3278 attached to a MVS system) It does you little good to have a program that does fancy screen I/O if it cannot be ported to another platform (unless, of course, it is strictly intended for only one platform)

Simplest C program possible: Part II
full ANSII compatability with no compiler warnings or errors

```c
void main (void): /* prototype for main, usually not required, but guaranteed
                     to work with all ANSI compilers */
void main( )
{
}
```

OR

```c
/* ANSI header stating return type * /
int main(void); /* prototype for main, usually not required, but guaranteed
to work with all ANSI compilers */
int main ( )
{
    return 0;
}
```

prog6.c   mathematics operators, precedence

```
main ( )

{
        /* declare four integers and space for answers */
        int a = 1; int b = 2; int c = 3; int d = 4; int ans;
        /* precedence of - + *
         ( ) parentheses
        -       unary minus    +       unary plus
        ++      increment      --      decrement
        *       multiplication
        /       division
        %       modulo
        +       addition                - subtraction
        ==      equality                = equals    */

        /* print initial values */
        printf("a => %i \t b => %i \t c => %i \t d => %i \n\n",a,b,c,d);

        /* subtraction example */
        ans = a - b;
        printf("a - b = %i \n",ans);

        /* precedence problem, want addition then multiplication */
        ans = a + b * c;
        printf("a + b * c = %i \n",ans);

        /* precedence example */
        ans = ( a + b ) * c;
        printf("( a + b ) * c = %i \n",ans);
}
```

/* sample output */

a => 1   b=> 2   c=>3   d=>4

a – b = -1

a + b * c = 7

(a + b) * c = 9

prog7.c   mixed mode arithmetic

/* program demonstrates mathematics, precedence and the difference between integer division */

/* how value is stored is determined by destination data type */

/* and floating division *}

```c
main ( )
{
        /* declare and initialize
        integers */ int a = 7; int b = 2;
        int int_ans;
         /* declare and initialize floats */
        float c = 7.0; float d = 2.0; float float ans;
        /* print initial values */
        printf("a => %i \t b => %i \t c => %f\t d =>
%f\n\n",a,b,c,d);
        printf("integer divided by integer
        \n");
        intans = a / b;
        printf("%i / %i = %i \n\n",a,b,int_ans);
        printf("float divided by float
        \n");
        float ans = c / d;
        printf("%f / %f = %f\n\n",c,d,float_ans);
        intans = c /
        b;
        floatans = c
        / b;
        printf("float divided by integer \n");
        printf(" stored in integer %f / %i = %i
        \n",c,b,int_ans);
        printf(" stored in float %f / %i =
%f\n\n",c,b,float_ans);
```

```
printf("integer divided by a float
\n");
int_ans = a / d;
float_ans = a / d;
printf(" stored in integer %i / %f = %i
\n",a,d,ineans);
printf(" stored in float %i / %f =
%f\n\n",a,d,floaeans);

printf(("-a = %i \n",-a);
printf("-c = %f\n",-c);
}
```

sample output

a => 7 b => 2   C => 7.000000 d => 2.000000

integer divided by integer

7/2 = 3   .;

float divided by float

7.000000 / 2.000000 = 3.500000

float divided by integer

 stored in integer 7.000000 / 2 = 3

 stored in float 7.000000 /2 = 3.500000

 integer divided by a float

 stored in integer 7 /2.000000 = 3

 stored in float 7 /2.000000 = 3.500000

 -a =-7

-c = -7.000000

prog8.c the modulus (remainder, residue) operator

```
/* the modulus operator only works on whole numbers*/
main ( )
{
        int guzinta;
        int rem;
        guzinta = 25 /5;
        rem = 25 % 5;
        printf("5 goes into 25 %i times with remainder %i \n",guzinta, rem);
        guzinta = 25 / 7;
        rem = 25 % 7;
        printf("7 goes into 25 %i times with remainder %i \n",guzinta.rem);
}
```

output you'll see

5 goes into 25 5 times with remainder 0

7 goes into 25 3 times with remainder 4

Exercise 3

/* Part 1 */

/* write a program that evaluates the following expression */

/* display the result in integer format */

/*

        ans = 7 times 9 plus 19 divided by 5 modulo 2

        do the multiplication first

            the division second

            the modulo third

            and the addition last

*/

/* Part 2 */

/* write a program that evaluates the following expression */

/* use exponential formats for the numbers */

/* display the result in exponential format */

/* (.000000097 + 2010) / (89000 * 23) */

Solution for Exercise 3

```c
main ( )
{
        int ans;
        float a,b,c,d;
        float numerator;
        float denominator;
        float result;

        a = 9.7e-8;
        b = 2.01e3;
        c = 8.9e4;
        d = 23.0;

        ans = ( 7 * 9 ) + ( ( 19/5 ) % 2);
        printf("ans = %i \n",ans );
        numerator = a + b;
        denominator = c * d;
        printf("numerator = %e \n",numerator);
        printf("denominator = %e \n",denominator);
        result = numerator / denominator;
        printf("Result = %e \n",result);
}
```

Relational (Comparison) Operators

<	less than
>	greater than
==	equivalent to
<=	less than or equivalent to
>=	greater than or equivalent to
!=	not equivalent to

Relational operators are used in relational expressions. A relational expression is defined as anything that can produce a True or False answer. Falsity is defined as zero. Truth is defined as non-zero. A variable by itself can be a relational expression because its value will be examined to see if it is zero or non zero. A relational expression can exist by itself, it does not have to be examined within the context of a decision.

The relational operators return a 1 if true, 0 if false.

```
/* steve.c August 10, 1993 */
main ( )
{
        int x, y, z;
        y = 2;
        /* y = 3 is a relational expression * /
        /* its truth or falsity is assigned to x */
        x = y == 3; /* assign to x the result of the comparison */
        printf("AAA x = %i y = %i\n",x,y);


        y = 3;
        /* y == 3 is a relational expression * /
        /* its truth or falsity is assigned to x */
        x = y == 3;
        printf("BBB x = %i Y = %i\n",x,y);


        x == y; /* no side effect, return value not used, this does nothing */
        printf("CCC x = %i y = %i\n",x,y);
        x < y;
        printf("DDD x = %i y = %i\n",x,y);
        z = x < y;
        printf("EEE z = %i x = %i Y = %i\n",z,x,y);

/* sample output */
AAA x= O y = 2
BBB x = 1  y  = 3
CCC x = 1 y  = 3
DDD x = 1 y = 3
EEE z = 1 x = 1 Y = 3
```

Run this program through alint and see that it tells you that there are several bugs.

prog9a.c   three types of loops

```c
main ( )
{
        int sum;
        int n;
        /* sum and loop counter need to be initialized */
        sum = 0; n = -5;

    /* while (relational expression) */
    /* while loop, check condition at top */
    while ( n <= 5 )
    {
            sum = sum + n;
            n = n + 1;
            printf("n is %i sum is %i \n",n,sum);
    }
    printf("WHILE LOOP:sum is %i \n\n\n",sum);

    /* do loop, check condition at bottom */
    sum = 0; n = -5;
    do
    {
            sum = sum + n;
            n = n + 1;
            printf("n is %i sum is %i \n",n,sum);
    } while ( n, <= 5 );
    printf("DO LOOP:sum is %i \n\n\n",sum);

    /* for loop, C shorthand to get all loop things on one line */
    for ( sum = 0, n = -5; n <= 5; n++ )
    {
            sum = sum + n;
    }
    /* print out the results */
    printf("FOR LOOP:sum is %i \n\n",sum);
}
```

prog10.c for loop

```c
/* program to calculate squares */
main ( )
{
        int square;
        int n;
        printf("TABLE OF SQUARES NUMBERS \n\n");
        printf("\t n \t n squared\n");
        printf("\t---\t----------\n");
        for ( n = 1; n <= 20; n++ )
        {
                square = n * n;
                printf("\t %i \t %i \n",n,square);
        }        \t is the tab character
}
```

TABLE OF SQUARES NUMBERS

n	n squared
1	1
2	4
3	9
4	16
5	25
6	36
7	49
8	64
9	81
10	100
11	121
12	144
13	169
14	196
15	225
16	256
17	289
18	324
19	361
20	400

Comparison of Loop Syntax

For a = 1 to 37 by 2

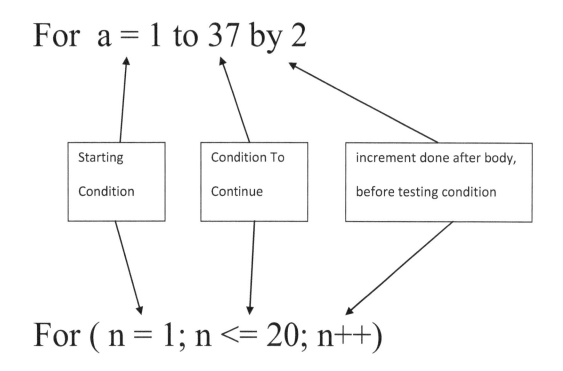

| Starting Condition | Condition To Continue | increment done after body, before testing condition |

For (n = 1; n <= 20; n++)

n is initialized to 1   // n = 1

perform test,   // if n <= 20

    if true, do body

    if false, skip body

after body performed, do increment //n++

Exercise:
with

Rewrite the previous example (progl0.c) and replace the for loop

a while loop, and then a do-while loop.

Exercise:

Make the previous program do the table of squares from 10 to 50
by 2's. i.e, 10 12 14 16 ...

Exercise:

Make the previous program do the table of squares from 33 to -7
by -3's i.e. 33, 30,27,24 ...

prog11.c   for loop   scanf input

```
/* program to calculate squares * /
/* introduces scanf for user
  input */
main ( )
{
        int square;
        int cube;
        int n;
        int user number;
        printf("How far do you want to go to? \n");
        scanf("%i",&user_number);
        printf("\nYou entered %i \n\n",user_number);
        printf("TABLE OF SQUARES & CUBES\n\n");
        printf("\t n \t n squared \t n cubed\n");
        printf("\t---\t-----------\t ---------\n");
        for (n = 1; n <= user_number; n++)
        {
                square = n * n;
                cube = square * n;
                printf("\t %i \t %i \t\t %i\n",n,square,cube);
        }
}
/* EXERCISE: remove the & from &user_number, you will experience a core  dump.
This is because scanf requires the & on the variable to read the data into. It needs to be
passed the address of where to write to */
/* UNIX PROGRAMMER'S HINT: when you have a program with a scanf
            in it,
            do a grep on the file with the scanf as the string to search for.
            Double check that every scanf has an & associated with it. If you
            know C shell programming, make a shell script to do the grep and
            print only the lines that have scanfs and not & */
```

If the & is left off, and if you use the highest warning level, the compiler should warn you that

you are trying to use the value of the variable user_number before it has been set.
TRY TO GET INTO THE HABIT OF READING ALL WARNINGS FROM THE COMPILER! IT IS CONSIDERED GOOD PRACTICE THAT YOUR PROGRAM WHEN 'DONE' SHOULD CAUSE NO WARNINGS.

EXERCISE: see how large a number you can input and still get the square and cube of. Try to make the integer result go out of range

SCANF "Feature" or "Bug"

scanf always leaves a carriage return in the input stream. If you are mixing line input via scanf and character input via getchar, you will have to eat the carriage return left behind by the scanf or you will have to flush the input stream

89	cr	23	cr	'p'	cr

Using scanf for Input

scanf(" format_specifier" , address of variable to satisfy format_specifier);

prog12.c nested for loops

"Ukranian doll for loops" "Matreshka"

```c
/* program to calculate squares */
/* introduces nested for loop */
main ( )
{
        int square, n, user_number, counter, i;
        /* this loop will be done four times */
        /*  counter will take on the values, 1 234 */
        for (counter = 1; counter < 5; counter++ )
        {
                printf("How far do you want to go to? \n");
                scanf("%i",&user_number);
                printf("\tYou entered %i \n\n",user_number); /* \f form feed */
                printf("TABLE OF SQUARES \n\n");
                printf("\t n \t n squared\n");
                printf("\t---\t----------\n");
                /* this loop will be done user_number times */
                /* n will take on values 1 through user_number */
                for (n = 1; n <= user_number; n++ )
                {
                        square = n * n;
                        printf("\t %i \t %i \n",n,square);
                        } /* end of n loop */
        } /* end of counter loop */
        printf("\n\n");

        /*COMMON PROGRAMMING MISTAKES */
        for ( i = 0; i < 5; i++ )
        {
          printf("outer i = %i \n",i);
```

```c
        /* using same loop counter in a nested loop */
        for ( i = 6; i < 9; i++ )
         {
                printf("inner i = %i \n",i);
         }
        printf("\n\n");

        for ( i = 0; i < 5; i++ )
         {
                printf("outer i = %i \n",i);
                /* changing value of loop variable */
                i += 7;
         }
} /* end main */
```

Assume i and j are ints

What Would be Printed?

```
for ( i = 0; i < 5; i ++ )
{ for (j = 5; j > 3; j-- )
{
        printf("%i %i\n" .i.j);
   }
}
```

Assume x and m are ints

```
x = 5;
while ( x < 10) {
        m = x * 10;
        do {
                printf("%i %i \n" .x.m);
                m=m+ (m/2);
        } while ( m < 200 );
        x = x + 2;
}
```

prog13.c while loop

```
/* while loop */
/* introduces \a, ansi alert character*/
main ( )
{
        int i;
        int sum = 0;
        i = -5;
        while ( i <= 5 )
        {
                printf("\a i = %i \n",i);
                sum += i;
                i++;
        }
        printf("Sum from -5 to 5 is %i \n",sum);


        /* COMMON PROGRAMMING MISTAKE */
        /* Infinite LOOP */
        i = 1;
        EVERY C statement returns a value that may be used or ignored
        THE RETURN value of an assignment statement is the value assigned
        while ( i = 1 )
        {
                printf(" i = %i \n",i);
                i++;
                printf(" i = %i \n",i);
        }
    /*UNIX PROGRAMMER HINT */
    /* BEFORE COMPILING, AND ESPECIALLY BEFORE RUNNING */
    /*
                grep your file for all lines that have if, while, for in them
                double check that you have == where == is needed, and not =
```

many programmers replace == with some other defined value

see #define statement later

*/

/* add this line to top of program

#define MYEQ ==

then change the = in the while (i = 1) to while (i MYEQ 1) */

prog14.c while loop for secret number guessing

```
/* while loops */
/* program to ask for guesses until they get it right */
main ( )
{
        int guess = -1;
        int secret = 7;
        int count of guesses = 0;
        printf("Try to pick a number from 1 to 10 \n");

        /* possible infinite loop if user is real idiot */
        while ( guess != secret)
        {
                count of guesses++:
                printf("Enter a guess \n");
                scanf ("%i",&guess);
                printf("\n You entered %i \n" ,guess);
        } /* end while */
        printf("You got it after %i tries \n",count_of_guesses);

}
```

prog15.c   while loop vs. do loop

```
/* program to let user guess secret number */
/* shows difference between while loop and do
loop */
main ( )
{
        int guess;
        int secret = 7;
        int count_of_guesses = 1;
        printf("Try to pick a number from 1 to 10 \n");
        /* possible infinite loop if user is real idiot */
        /* need to preinitialize value for while loop */
        printf("Enter guess #%i\n",count_oCguesses);
        scanf ("%i",&guess);
        printf("\n You entered %i \n" ,guess);
        while ( guess ! = secret)
        {
                printf("WRONG\n");

                CONTROL will return from the system statement when the entire
                command has been completed. IF THE command was placed in the
                background
                control will return as soon as the placement has occurred

                system ("usr/demo/SOUND/play lusr/demo/SOUND/sounds/laugh.au");
                count_ of_guesses++:
                printf("Enter guess
                #%i\n",count_of_guesses);
                scanf ("%i",&guess);
                printf("\nYou entered %i \n",guess);
        } /* end while */
        printf("You got it after %i tries \n",count_oCguesses);
```

```c
printf("Try to pick a number from 1 to 10 \n");
count_of_guesses = 0;
secret = 3;
/* do not need to preinitialize value for do loop */
do
{
        count_of_guesses++;
        printf("Enter guess
        #%i\n",count_of_guesses);
        scanf ("%i",&guess);
        printf("\n You entered %i \n" ,guess);
        if ( guess !=
        secret)
        {
                printf("WRONG\n");
                system ("/usr/demo/SOUND/play
                /usr/demo/SOUND/sounds/laugh.au");
} while ( guess != secret );
printf("You got it after %i tries
\n",count_of_guesses);

}
```

Exercise 4

/* write a program to compute and print the first ten

  * /

 /* factorial numbers */

 /* desired output is a table */

/* 1! 1 */

/*2! 2 */

/*3! 6 */

/*   ...   */

/* 10! 3628800 */

If your program is more than 15 lines(of code, not counting comments) it is going the

wrong

direction.

HINT: mathematical identity N! = (N-I)! * N

Solution for Exercise 4

main ( )

```
{
        int i, factorial;
        factorial = 1;


        for ( i = 1; i <= 10; i++)
        {
                factorial = factorial * i;
                printf("%i!/t%i\n",i, factorial);
        }
}
```

Exercise 5

/* write a c program to input an integer as an integer* /

/* print out the number, one digit per line */

/* i.e. input 1234 */

/*   output 4 */

/*   3 */

/*   2 */

/*   1 */

Solution for Exercise 5

```c
main( )
{
        int i;
        int outnum;
        printf("Input number please \n");
        scanf("%i" ,&i);
        while (i > 0)
        {
                outnum = i % 10;
                printf("%i\n" ,outnum);
                i = i / 10;
        }
}
```

C   if   if else

if .c

```
main ( )
{
        int i;
        printf("enter a number \n");
        scanf("%i",&i);

        if (i < 100)
         {
                printf("%i is less than one hundred \n",i);
         }
        printf("After the first if statement\n");

        if (i < l0)
        {
                printf("%i is less than ten \n",i);
        }
        else
        {
                printf("%i is greater than or equal to ten\n",i);
        }
}
if ( relationalexpression )
 {
        execute if re TRUE
        ...
 }
 else /* must follow immediately */
 {
        execute if re FALSE
 }
```

prog16.c   math.h include file

```c
/* if statement */
/* math.h contains mathematical functions like sqrtO */
#include <math.h>
main ( )
{
        float number;
        float square_root;
        printf("\n\nType in a number \n");
        scanf("%f",&number);
        printf("\nYou entered %f\n",number);
        if ( number < 0 )
        {
                printf("Can't get square root of negative number \n");
        }
        else
        {
                square_root = sqrt(number);
                printf("The square root of %f is %f\n",number,square_root);
        }
        printf("Program completed \n");
}
/* EXERCISE remove the #include <math.h> line and see what you get */
/* some (but not all) of the math functions available
   for a complete list, consult your compiler's documentation
        ceil(x) floor(x)
        sin(x) cos(x) tan(x) asin(x) acos(x) atan(x)
        sinh(x) cosh(x) tanh(x)
        exp(x) log (x) loglO(x) pow(x,y)
*/
```

prog19.c logical operators and relational expressions

/* precedence of logical operators and brackets * /

```
/*
<       less than
<=      less than or equal to
>       greater than
>=      greater than or equal to
==      equality
!+      inequality
&&      logical and
||      logical or


main ( )
    {
            int score;
            printf("Enter the score\n");
            scanf("%i",&score);
            printf("You entered %i\n",score);
            if ( score < 0 || score> 100 )
                    printf("Impossible score\n");
            else
            {
                if ( score >= 0 && score < 50 )
                        printf("F\n");
                else
                {
                        if ( score >= 50 && score < 70)
                                printf("D\n");
                        else
                        {
                                if ( score >= 70 && score < 80)
```

```c
                printf("C\n");
        else if ( score >= 80 && score < 90)
                printf("B\n");
        else if (score >= 90 && score <= 100)
                printf("A\n");
        else
                printf("no way to get here \n");
        }
    }
  }
}
```

if (relational expression)

relational expression evaluates to TRUE or FALSE

if ((r e 1) || (r e 2))

|| is the logical or operator

re1	re2	result
t	t	t
t	f	t
f	t	t
f	f	f

if (relational expression)

relational expression **evaluates to TRUE or FALSE**

if ((re1) && (re2))

&& is the logical and operator

rel	re2	result
t	t	t
t	f	f
f	t	f
f	f	f

prog20.c complex decision structures

```c
#define      IBM   1
#define      MER   2
#define      MMD   3
#define      QUIT  4
 main ( )
 {
      int stock symbol;
      char p_or_c;
      char cr;

      printf("\nEnter stock symbolI\n");
      printf(" 1       IBM\n");      printf("2 MER \n");
      printf("3       MMD\n");      printf("4 QUIT \n");
      scanf("%i",&stock_symbol );
      scanf("%c",&cr);
      printf("You entered %i\n",stock_symbol);

      if ( stock symbol == IBM )
            printf("%.2f\n",53.25);
       else if ( stock_symbol == MER)
            printf("%.2f\n",71.75);
       else if ( stock_symbol == QUIT )
            printf("YOU SELECTED QUIT\n");
       else if ( stocksymbol == MMD )
       {
            printf("(P)referred or (C)ommon?\n");
            scanf("%c",&p_or_c );
            scanf("%c",&cr);
             if (p_or_c == 'P' )
              {
                     printf("Preffered 22.5\11");
```

73

```c
            }
        else if (p_or_c == 'c' )
            {
                printf("Common 21.25\11");
        else
                printf("Unknown character \n");
    }
    else
    printf("Unknown symbol\n");
}
```

```
switch (discreet valued variable)
{
        case discreet value:
                        •••
                        •••
                        break;
        case discreet value:
                        •••
                        •••
                        break;
        •••
        •••
        default:
                        •••
                        •••
                        break;
}
```

prog21.c switch statement

```c
#include <string.h>
#include <ctype.h>
#define        IBM    1
#define        MER    2
#define        MMD    3
#define        QUIT   4


int stock_symbol;
char p_or_c;
char cr;


printf("\nEnter stock symbol\n");
printf(" 1        IBM\n");
printf("2        MER\n");
printf("3        MMD\n");
printf("4        QUTI\n");
scanf("%i",&stock_symbol );
scanf("%c",&cr);
printf("You entered %i\n",stock_symbol);


switch ( stock_symbol )
{
        case IBM:
                printf("%.2f\n",53.25);
                break;
        case MER:
                printf("%.2f\n" ,71.75);
                break;
        case QUIT:
                printf("YOU SELECTED QUI1\n");
                break;
```

```c
            caseMMD:

printf("(P)referred or (C)ommon?\n");
scanf("%c",&p_occ);
scanf("%c",&cr);
            if (toupper(p_or_c) == 'P' ) /* this is an **atrocious** line of code */
                                    /* can you figure out why? */
        {
            printf("Preffered 22.5\11");
        }
        else if (toupper(p_or_c) == 'C' ) /* ATROCIOUS */
        {
            printf("Common 21.25\n");
        }
        else
            printf("Unknown character\n");
            break;
    default:
        printf("Unknown symbol\n");
} /* end switch */


/* Exercise, remove the break in case IBM, what happens? Why? */
```

THESE TWO LINES ARE ATROCIOUS, yet common.

Why?

(toupper is a macro that converts a character to its upper case equivalent)

Exercise 6

/* write a program to have a person guess a secret number.

Let the range of valid numbers be zero to 100.

Let them have a maximum of 7 tries.

Tell them if they were too high or too low.

Report the remaining range of possiblities for them */

Solution for Exercise 6

```c
main ( )

{
        int secret;
        int guess;
        int
        num_guesses
        = 0;
        int hi = 100;
        int lo = 0;
        int seed;

        printf("What time is it hh:mm:ss\n");
        scanf("%i:%i:%i",&seed,&seed,&seed);
        srand( seed);   /* random number function */
        secret = (int) rand() / 330;
          if ( secret < 0 )
          secret = 0;
        if (secret> 100 )
          secret = 100;

        /* make sure that guess is incorrect to begin with
*/
        guess = secret - 1;
        while ( (secret != guess) && (num guesses
        < 7) )
        {
                num_guesses++;
                prfntf("Enter a guess between %i and %i\n",hi,lo);
                scanf("%i", &guess);
                printf("\nYou entered %i\n",guess);
                if ( guess <
```

```c
                           secret)
    {
                system ("/usr/demo/SOUND/play
                /usr/demo/SOUND/sounds/laugh.au");
                printf("TOO LOW\n");
                if ( guess > lo )
                        lo = guess;
            else if ( guess > secret)
            {
                system ("/usr/demo/SOUND/play
                /usr/demo/SOUND/sounds/laugh.au");
                printf("TOO HIGH\n");
                if ( guess < hi )
                        hi = guess;
            }
        }
    }
}
```

Exercise 7

/* FOR THE MATHEMATICALLY INCLINED */

/* write a program to solve for the real roots of */
/* the quadratic equation ax^2 + bx + c */
/* input a , b , c */
/* check for real or imaginary roots */
/* make sure not to divide by zero */
/* test data   1 2 1   => single real root   x1 = -1 */
/*   1 -1 -6   => two real roots x1 = -2, x2 = 3 */
/*   0 0 0   => one real root   x1 = 0 */
/*   0 4 -2   => one real root   x1 = .5 */

x1 = -1
x1 = -2, x2 = 3
x1 = 0
x1 = .5

Solution for Exercise 7

```c
#include <math.h>
main ( )
{
        float a, b, c;
        float discriminant;
        float xl, x2;

        printf("\n\ninput a b and c separated by spaces \n");
        scanf("%f %f %f",&a,&b,&c);
        printf("you entered %f %f %f\n\n\n",a,b,c);
        discriminant = ( b * b) - ( 4 * a * c);
        if ( discriminant> 0 )
        {
            if (a == 0)
            {
              if ( b == 0 )
              {
                        printf("x = 0 \n");
              else
              {
                        xl = (-c)/b;
                        printf("Single real root is %f\n",xl);
              }
            }
            else
            {
                    xl = ( -b + sqrt(b*b - 4*a*c)) / (2 * a);
                    x2 = ( -b - sqrt(b*b - 4*a*)) / ( 2 * a);
                    printf("Two real roots are \n");
                    printf("%f %f\n",xl,x2);
```

```c
    }

    else if ( discriminant == 0 )
    {
        printf("one real root \n");
        if (a == 0 )
         {
            x1 = 0;
            printf("x1 = %f\n",x1);
         }
        else
         {
            x1 = -b / (2*a);
            printf("x1 = %f\n",x1);
         }else
    {
        printf("Imaginary Roots\n");
    }
    printf("\n\n");
}/* end program */
```

Exercise 8

/* exercise for those who don't want to do quadratic equations */

/* write a C program that:

       inputs an integer number from the keyboard

       displays it forwards

       displays it backwards */

/* big, brain buster

       as you reverse the number, print out each digit on a

       seperate line, with the english language word beside the digit */

/* humungous brain destroyer

       print out the english word for the number as a whole

       i.e. 653 => six hundred fifty three

*/

Solution for Exercise 8

```c
/* write a c program to input an integer */
/* print out the number, one digit per line */
/* i.e. input 1234 */
/*      output 4
            3
            2
            1 */                .
/* then print it out in reverse order */
/* then print the english word beside each digit */
char * words[] = { "Zero", "Un", "Deux", "Trois", "Quatre", "Cinq", "Six",
"Sept", "Huit", "Neuf"};


/* solution */
main ( )
 {
        int
        i,safe,outnum;
        int revnum = 0;
        printf("Input number \n");
        scanf("%i",&i);
        while (i > 0)
        {
                outnum = i % 10;              /* strip off last digit */
                revnum = revnum * 10 + outnum;
                printf("%i \n",outnum); /* print it */
                i = i /10;                    /* divide current number by 10
                                              effectively dropping last digit */
        safe = revnum;
        printf("\n\n");
```

```c
        while ( revnum > 0 )
        {
                outnum = revnum % 10;  /* strip off last digit */
                printf("%i \n",outnum);  /* print it */
                revnum /= 10;
        }
        printf("\n\n");


/* now print digit by digit with english words */
while (safe > 0 )
{
        outnum = safe % 10; /* strip off last digit */
        printf("%i\t",outnum); /* print it*/
        printf(" % s\t",words [outnum]);

        switch( outnum)
        {
                case 0:
                        printf("Zero\n");
                        break;
                case 1:
                        printf("One\n");
                        break;
                case 2:
                        printf("Two\n");
                        break;
                case 3:
                        printf("Three\n");
                        break;
                case 4:
                        printf ("Four");
                        break;
                case 5:
```

```c
                printf("Five\n");
                break;
        case 6:
                printf("Six\n");
                break;
        case 7:
                printf("Seven\n);
                break;
        case 8:
                printf("Eight\n");
                break;
        case 9:
                printf("Nine\n"); break;
        }
        safe /= 10; /* divide current number by 10 */
    }
}
```

errors.c

```c
/* putting a semi colon after a definition */
#define MAX_VALUE              100;


/* forgetting that upper and lower case matter */
#define ONE 0;
main ( ) {
        int j = 200; int k = 0;
        /* adding a semi-colon where there shouldn't be one */
    if( j ==  100);  ◄─────────────────────────────
            printf("J = 100\n");
        /* leaving off a semi-colon where there should be one */


        /* won't compile because of #if 0 */
#if 0
    if( j ==  100)
    /* missing a semi-colon where you need one */
            printf("l = 100\n")  ◄──────────────────────
    else
            printf("J not equal to 100 \n");


      /* using one = where you need two == */
◄───────────────────────────────
    if (j = MAX_VALUE )
            printf("J was equal to MAX_ VALUE\n");
#endif
        /* putting = instead of == in a conditional */
        if(j = 1)  ◄─────────────────────────
            printf("J was equal to 1 \n");


        /* not using parantheses on math and forgetting */
        /* the precedence of operations */
        j = 1 + 2 - 3 * 4/ 5 / 6 * 7 - 8 + 9;
```

88

```
        primf("J = %d \n",j);
#if 0
        j =  One;
        printf("j = %d \n",j);
#endif
        /* forgetting the & character in scanf calls will cause core dump */
        printf("Enter value for j \n");
        scanf("%i", j);
        printf("You entered %i\n",j);
```

Here is a line of code actually found in a 'real' delivered product:

if (length = 8) length == 7; /* if length is 8 reset it to 7 */

it was quite interesting to determine what if anything to do with or about this ..

What would you have done??

prog22.c simple array

```c
/* introduces simple array */
/* note that indexing goes from 0 to 4 */
/* declaration syntax indicates 5 cells */
/* starting at index 0 */
main( )
{
        int array1[5];
        int i;
        array1[0] = 23;
        array1[1] = 17;
        array1[2] = 29;
        array1[3] = 3;
        array1[4] = -7;
        for ( i = 0; i <= 4; i++ )
        {
                printf("array1[%i] = %i \n",i,array1[i]);
        }
        /*
        array1[0] = 23
        array 1 [1] = 17
        array1[2] = 29
        array 1 [3] = 3
        array 1 [4] =-7
        */
```

Arrays: Discussion

To declare an array we state the type of its elements, the name of the array, and the number of elements in it:

int arl[l0];

defines storage for an array of 10 integers called arl.

Since all calls in C are call by value, what is the value of arl if we were to pass it to a function?

Mentioning arl with no subscript is to mention its address. This means the address of the first element in the array. When an array is subscripted, like: ar[1] = 42; what actually happens is this, the compiler generates the code to take the starting address of the array (the address of the zero-th element, arl), adds the size of 1 integer to it (to get the address of the element at location 1 in the array) and 'goes to' that address. In this case we are doing an assignment operation, so the correct code is generated to perform a memory store at that address.

Since the compiler generates the address in this way, it assumes the programmer has verified that the resulting address will be correct. **There are no array bounds checking in C, neither at compile nor at run time!** Part of the reason for this is to maximize execution speed, the other is that the authors wish to place the responsibility for (orrectness upon the programmer at design time.

Other languages (like Pascal) enforce tight run-time checking.

Arrays may have more than 1 dimension:

int two_dim [2] [3l={ { 1,2,3 }, { 4,5,6} };

two_dim is a 2 by 3 array of integers. There are 2 rows of three columns.

Or we might say two_dim is an array of 2 3 integer arrays. In fact this is a better description as that is how it is stored remember, a 3 integer array is represented by its address. So two_dim has 2 entries in it each of which is the address where a 3 integer array begins in memory.

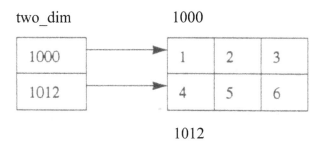

The statement two_dim[1][2] = 42; is compiled as:

Take the address in two_dim[1], add 2 integer sizes to it and go to that address and assign the

value 42 (1012 + (2 * 4) = 1020 the address of the third item in the second row)

prog23.c array boundaries

```
main( )
{
        int array1[5] = { 23, 17, 29, 3, -7 };


        /* print out values in array */
        for (i = 0- i <= 4- i++)
                printf("arrayl[%i] = %i \n",i,arrayl[i]);


        /* print out values in array and beyond boundaries of array */
                for ( i = -4; i < 10; i++ )
                printf("arrayl[%i] = %i \n",i,arrayl[i]);
}
/* sample output */
array 1 [0] = 23
array1[1] = 17
array1[2] = 29
array1[3] = 3
array 1 [4] =-7
array 1 [-4] = 3
array1[-3] = 16
array1[-2] = -2130509557
array1[-1] = -1
arrayl[0] = 23
array 1 [1] = 17
array1[2] = 29
array1[3] = 3
array 1 [4] =-7
array1[5] = 0
array 1 [6] = 0
array 1 [7] = 0
arrayl[8] = 0
array 1 [9] = 0
```

prog25.c   more array boundaries

```
/* note that values are assigned beyond declared space */
main ( )
{
            int array 1[5];
            int i;

            /* valid initialization */
            arrayl[0] = 23;
            arrayl[1]=l7;
            array1[2] = 29;
            arrayl[3] = 3;
            arrayl[4] = -7;

            /* these values are stored but can't be addressed
            */
            /* you can read from them but you can't write to
            them */
            /* because they are not part of your data space */
            x = array 1 [5] = 24;
            array1[6] = 9848;
            array1[7] =-38495;

            for ( i = 0; i <= 7; i++ )
                    printf("arrayl[%i] = %i \n",i,arrayl[i]);
/*sample
output
array 1 [0]
= 23
arrayl[l] =
17
array 1 [2]
= 29
array 1 [3]
= 3
arrayl[4]
=-7
arrayl [5] =
0
arrayl[6] =
0
array1[7] =
0
*/
```
QUESTION? Will x be set to 24 or 0?
Answer!   24, even though array 1 [5] is not set!
NOTE: on some systems (DOS for example) arrayl[5] may have been set to 24.
BEWARE: indexing outside array bounds can be very dangerous and causes many

headaches for both new and seasoned C programmers. Sometimes this is refered to as having a "wayward pointer" meaning storing or retrieving data from who-knows-where. These can be particularly nasty bugs to debug. In this example storing at arrayl[5] will quite possibly overwrite the variable i. On many systems storing a value at arrayl[-l] will cause an addressing exception (mainframe).

prog26.c bowling scores, array processing

```c
/* program to calculate the average of a set of bowling scores */
/* only count scores over 100 for person's average */
/* print out the high and low scores, all scores, scores used in average*/
/* print out average */
#define      MAX_SCORES        100
#define      MAX_SCORE         300
#define      MIN_SCORE         0
#define      MIN_LEAGUE_SCORE        100
main ( )
{
        /* scores will be the array of scores entered */
        int scores[MAX_SCORES];
        /* numscores is the count of how many scores they want to enter */
        int numscores, i, score;

        /* scores_to_count are used to keep track of how many valid scores there were */
        int raw_scores_to_count = 0;
        int league_scores_to_count = 0;
        int score_total = 0;

        /* the averages are floats because I want floating point accuracy */
        float raw_average;
        float league_average;

        /* initialize current high and low score */
        int high = 0;
        int low = MAX_SCORE;

        /* find out how many scores the person will be entering */
        printf("How many scores will you be entering?");
        scanf("%i", &numscores);
```

```c
printf("\nYou entered %d scores \n",numscores);
if ( numscores > MAX_SCORES)
{
        printf("CANNOT TAKE THAT MANY, %i is max\n",MNCSCORES);
        exit(-1);
}
}

/* for each of the scores requested, get the score */
for (i = 1; i <= numscores; i++ )
{
        printf(,'\nEnter score #%i: ",i);
        sc anf(" % i" ,&score );
        printf("You entered %i\n",score);
        /* if scores was less than 100 * /
        /* don't count in average */
        if ( ( score < MIN_SCORE ) || ( score> MAX_SCORE))
                printf("Impossible score \n");
        else
        {
                /* insert score into array */
                scores [raw _scores_to_count] = score;

                /* update the total of all scores */
                score_total = score_total + score;
                raw _scores~to_count++;

                if ( score > high)
                        high = score;
                if ( score < low)
                        low = score;
} /* end for loop */
if ( raw _scores_to_count > 0 )
{
```

```c
            raw_average = score_total/raw_scores_to_count;
            printf("\nRaw average = %.2f\n", raw_average);
            printf("High score was %i \n",high);
            printf("Low score was %i \n",low);
    }
    else
            printf("No valid scores entered\n");


    score_total = 0;
    league_scores_to_count = 0;
    printf("\n\nLIST OF LEAGUE SCORES USED IN AVERAGE\n");
    for ( i= 0; i < raw_scores_to_count; i++ )
    {
            if (scores[i] > MIN_LEAGUE_SCORE )
            {
                    printf("\t%i\n" ,scores [i]);
                    league_scores_to_count++;
                    score_total += scores[i];
    if ( league_scores_to_count > 0 )
    {
            league_average = score_total / league_scores_to_count;
            printf("\nLeague average = %.2f\n",league_average);
    else
            league_average = 100;
} /*end main */
```

How many scores will you be entering?

You entered 10 scores

Enter score #1: You entered 100

Enter score #2: You entered 200

Enter score #3: You entered 300

Enter score #4: You entered - 3

Impossible score

Enter score #5: You entered 50

Enter score #6: You entered 100

Enter score #7: You entered 200

Enter score #8: You entered 300

Enter score #9: You entered 79

Enter score #10: You entered 407

Impossible score

Raw average = 166.12

High score was 300

Low score was 50

LIST OF LEAGUE SCORES USED IN AVERAGE

    200

    300

    200

    300

League average = 250.00

prog27.c character arrays

&s address of s

s value of s

*s value stored at address stored in s

/* program to illustrate initializing a character array */

/* will be initialized three different ways */

/* null terminator is added to word1 */

/* size of wordl would be determined at initialization time*/

int i,t;

char wordl[] =

{"abcdefghij"};

main ( )

{

       char word3[] = {"12345678901234 56789"};

       /* null terminator is not added to word2 */

       /* size of word2 would be determined at initialization

       time*/

       char word2[] = { 'H', 'e', 'l', 'l', 'O', '!' };

       char word4[] = {"ABCDEFGHIJKLMNOP"};

       /* null terminator is added to s size of s is size of pointer to char * /

       /* space for s is allocated at initialization time since the thing in double quotes

              must be stored somewhere The space for character string is made on

              stack */

       char * s = {"still yet another way, pointer to character"};

       for (i = 0; i < 20; i++)

            printf("%c %x\n", wordl[i],

word1[i]);

printf("\n");

/* this is a really terrible thing to do, calling a subroutine over and over

       each time it is called it returns the same value. */

```c
for ( i = 0; i < sizeof(word1); i++ )
        printf("%c", word 1 [i]);
printf("\n");


printf("%s",word1); /* this is much
better */
printf("\n") ;
for (i = 0; i < 20; i++ )
        printf("%c %x\n",
word2[i],word2[i]);
printf("\n");


t = sizeof(word2);
printf("sizeof word2 is %i
\n",t);
for ( i = 0; i < t; i++ )
        printf("%c", word2[i]);
printf("\n");
printf("%s", word2);
printf("\n");


for ( i = 0; i < 20; i++ )
        printf("%c",s[i]);
printf("\n");


for ( i = 0; i < sizeof(s); i++ )
        printf("%c",s[i]);
printf('\n");


for ( i = 0; i < sizeof(*s); i++ )
        printf("%c" ,s[i]);
printf("\n");
printf("%s",s);
```

```
        printf("\n") ;
}
```

Output You'll See

a 61
b62
c 63
d64
e 65
f66
g 67
h 68
i 69
j 6a
0
1 31
2 32
3 33
4 34
5 35
6 36
7 37
8 38
9 39

abcdefghij
abcdefghij
H 48
e 65
l6 c
1 6c
o 6f
! 21
1 31
2 32
3 33
4 34
5 35
6 36
7 37
8 38
9 39
0 30
1 31
2 32
3 33
4 34
 sizeof word2 is 6
 Hello!
 Hello! 1234567890123456789
 still yet another wa
 stil
 s
 still yet another way, pointer to character

Exercise 9

/* write a program to input a list of numbers into an array */

/* print the array elements forwards and backwards */

/*

Write a program to input a list of numbers into an array

Find the largest element of the array

Find the smallest element of the array

Put the smallest value at position 0 in the array and

put the value that was at position 0 where the

smallest value used to be

Print out the updated array */

Solution for Exercise 9

```
int main ( )
{
        int array[l0] = {1, 3,5, -2, -6, 7, 4, 9, 12,932 };
        int i, hipos, lopos, temp;
        hipos = lopos = 0;
        printf("Original Array \n");
        for ( i = 0; i < 10; i++ )
        {
                printf("Array position %i value %i
                'n",i,array[i]);
                if ( array[i] > array[hipos] )
                        hipos = i;
                if ( array[i] < array[lopos] )
                        lopos = i;
        }
        printf("Largest value is %i at index %i \n",array[hipos],hipos);
        printf("Smallest value is %i at index %i \n",array[10pos],lopos);

        /* switch lowest value to position 0, moving position 0 to where lowest came from
        */
        temp = array[lopos];
        array[lopos] = array[0];
        array[0] = temp;
        printf("Updated Array
        \n");
        for ( i  = 0; i < 10; i++
        )
                printf("Array position %i value %i
                'n",i,array[i]);
} /* end main */
```

Exercise 10

/* write a program to sort an array of
numbers */

/* use the array 1 35 -2 -67 49 12932 */

/* sort the array from low to high */

/* print out the original and the sorted array */

/* DO NOT use a second array to sort the numbers

into,

you have to sort them in the array they are

in */

Note: you may implement the sort however you are
comfortable

The following is pseudocode for the so-called bubble
sort:

(ASSUMES ZERO BASED INDEXING)

FOR INDEX1 IS 0 TO NUMBER OF ELEMENTS IN

ARRAY-1

(from first to second to last)

FOR INDEX2 IS INDEX1 +1 To NUMBER OF ELEMENTS IN ARRAY

(from second to last)

IF ELEMENT AT INDEX 1 IS GREATER THAN THE ELEMENT AT

INDEX2

SWAP ELEMENTS AT INDEX 1 AND INDEX2

ENDIF

ENDFOR

ENDFOR

Solution for Exercise 10

```c
main ( )

{
        int array[l0] = { 1,3,5, -2, -6, 7, 4, 9, 12,932 };
        int temp;
        int i,j;
        printf("Original unsorted array \n");
        for ( i = 0; i < 10; i++ )
        {
                printf("%i\t%i\n" ,i,array[i]);
        }
        for ( i = 0; i < 9; i ++ )
        {
                for (j = i + 1; j < 10; j++ )
                {
                        if ( array[j] < array [i] )
                        {
                                temp = arrayjj];
                                arrayjj] = array[i];
                                array[i] = temp;
                        } /* end if */
                } /* end for j loop */
        } /* end for i loop */
        printf("\n\nSorted Array\n");
        for ( i = 0; i < 10; i++ )
                printf("%i\t%i\n" ,i,arra y[i]);

}
```

Function definition and prototypes

When we #include <stdio.h> what happens? The file stdio.h gets imbeddeed into our program.

The file stdio.h contains the prototypes for functions like printf (and other stuff).

A prototype is a declaration of what the interface for a function looks like. For printf it is:

    unsigned printf(char *, ...);

This indicates that the printf function returns an unsigned int, and requires at least one argument, which must be a character string.

The compiler "remembers" the prototype after it "sees" it and will check our code to verify that

we are using it correctly. If we fail to pass printf at least a character string we will get a compiler

error. If we assign printf's return value to a non-unsigned, we will get at least a compiler warning.

When we write our own functions we will want to use prototypes to allow the compiler to provide the same type of checking as with printf.

If the compiler does not see a prototype for a function but sees it being used it will issue a warning and there will be no checking performed. This is deemed to be poor programming practice. We should always use prototypes to allow the compiler to verify our interfaces as well as our usage. A prototype is also known as a function declaration. To "declare" in C means to state that something exists (usually somewhere else).

The actual code for a function is called the function definition. To "define" in C means to create

code or storage.

Just as a note, many other languages support similar concepts as prototypes.

prog29.c elementary function declaration and usage

```
/* definition of subroutine */
/* should be defined before it is
used */
/* type of value it returns
     name
          type of arguments it expects */
/* program execution does not start here */
/* this code is only executed when the subrl routine is
called */
void subr1(void) /* this is called the function header */
 {
        printf("In
        subroutine\n");
        return;
 }
/* this is where program execution
starts */
main( )
 {
        /* declaring that main will call subr1 */
        /* function prototype header needs to go before first executable
        statement */
        void subr1(void);

        printf("In main
        routine \n");
        subr1( ):
        printf("Back in main routine \n");
}


/* sample output */
```

In main routine

In subroutine

Back in main routine

If we hadn't placed the prototype for subrl in main, the compiler by default woud assume that the function header correctly stated the return and parameter types. This only works because the compiler 'sees' the function definition in the same file as it is used. Again this is deemed poor style. If the definition for subrl was after main in the source file, we must place the prototype for subrl before it's use in main. Leaving out the prototype wouldn't work as the compiler would not see the header line before it was used.

prog30.c calling subroutines

```c
/* definition of subroutine */
/* should be defined before it is used */
/* type of value it returns
     name
           type of arguments it expects */
/* program execution does not start here */
/* this code is only executed when the subrl routine is called */
void subr1(void)
{
        printf("In subroutine\n");
        return;
}


/* this is where program execution starts */
main( )
{
        /* declaring that main will call subrlO */
        void subr1(void);
        printf("In main routine \n");
        subr1( );
        subr1( );
        subrl ( );
        printf("Back in main routine \n");
}
```

prog31.c passing constants to subroutines

```c
/* definition of subroutine, should be defined before it is used */
/* type of value it returns

    name

            type of arguments it expects */
/* program execution does not start here */
/* this code is only executed when the subrl routine is called */
void subr1(int n)  {
        /* n is a local variable (argument) who's purpose is to */
        /*  receive a copy of the parameter passed from main routine */
        /* i is a local variable it wil l live on stack */
        /* it will be deallocated when routine exits */
        int i;
        for ( i = 0; i < n; i++ )
                printf("In subroutine i = %i n = %i \n",i,n);
        return;
}
/* this is where program execution starts */
main( )
 {
        /* declaring that main will call subr1( ) */
        void subr1(int);
        printf("In main routine \n");
        /* calling subrl, sending 5 by value */
        subr1 (5);
        printf("Back in main routine \n");
 }
/* sample output */
In main routine
In subroutine i = 0 n = 5
In subroutine i = 1 n = 5
In subroutine i = 2 n = 5
In subroutine i = 3 n = 5
In subroutine i = 4 n = 5
Back in main routine
```

prog32.c passing variables to subroutines

```c
/* program execution does not start here */
/* this code is only executed when the subrl routine is called */
void subr1(int n)
{
        /* n is an argument passed from main routine, it is a local variable */
        /* i is a local variable, it will live on stack */
        /* it will be deallocated when routine exits, as will n */
        int i;
        /* static variable lives in data area, it's value */
        /* is retained between calls beware of static variables */
        /* in general, assume no static area is available */
        /* on some O/S, static variables are shared between all instances of the program */
        /* this defeats re-entrancy */
        static int j = 0;

        for ( i = 0; i < n; i++ )
        {
                j++;
                printf("In subroutine i = %d j = %d \n",i,j);
        }
        return;
/* this is where program execution starts */
main ( )
{
        int x;
        /* declaring that main will call subr1( ) */
        void subr1(int);
        x = 2; printf("In main routine x = %i \n",x);
        subr1(x);
        printf("Main routine location 1 x = %i \n\n",x);
```

113

```
    x = 3; printf("In main routine x = %i \n",x);
    subr1(x);
    printf("Main routine location 2 x = %i \n\n",x);


    x = -4; printf("In main routine x = %i \n",x);
    subr1(x);
    printf("Main routine location 3 x = %i \n\n",x);
}
/* EXERCISE */
/* WHAT WILL THE OUPUT BE ?? */
```

SOLUTION TO EXERCISE

In main routine x = 2

In subroutine i = 0 j = 1

In subroutine i = 1 j = 2

Main routine location 1 x = 2

In main routine x = 3

In subroutine i = 0 j = 3

In subroutine i = 1 j = 4

In subroutine **i** = 2 j = 5

Main routine location 2 x = 3

In main routine x = -4

Main routine location 3 x = -4

prog33.c subroutines returning values (void keyword)

```c
/* routine will return no value, expects to receive an integer, will call integer n */
void cube1 ( int n )
{int cube;   /* local variable for subroutine */
        cube = n * n * n;
        printf("Cube of %i is %i \n",n,cube);
        return;
}


/* routine returns an int, expects an integer, will call integer n */
int cube2 ( int n )
{
        int cube;   /* local variable for subroutine */
        cube = n * n * n;
        return(cube);
}
main( )
{
        /* function prototype headers, not calls to subroutines */
        void cube1 (int );
        int cube2 ( int );
        /* local variables for main */
        int input_value;
        int returned_value;
        printf("Enter number to calculate cube of\n");
        scanf("%i" ,&input_ value);
        printf("Calling cube1\n");
        /* there is no return value to catch */
        cube1(input value);

        printf("\nCalling cube2\n");
        /* there is a return value to catch */
        returned_value = cube2(input_value);
        printf("cube of %i is %i \n",inpuCvalue,returned_value);
}
```

A Few Words About Multi-Module Programs

In the 'normal' programming world, we typically will not have just 1 giant source file. It makes more sense to have a file containing the main function, and one or more other files that contain functions typically grouped by functionality. Consider the three files test1.c funs1.c and funs2.c

```
test1.c              funs1.c               funs2.c
void main ( )        void f1 ( )           void f3 ( )
{                    {                     {
     f1( );               f3 ( );                    some code
     f2 ( );         }                     }
}                    void f2 ( )
                     {
                             some code
                     }
```

Since main calls nand f2 it should have the prototypes for these functions available to it at compile time. Likewise, since f1 calls f3, it should have the prototype for f3 available to it. We could try to remember to do this. However, there is an easier way!

We can write our own header files (one or more):

myproto.h

void f1 (void);

void f2(void);

void f3(void);

Then we can load them all by using #include "myprot.h."

test1.c	funs1.c	funs2.c
#include "myproto.h"	#include "myproto.h"	#incluee "myproto.h"
void main ( )	void f1 ( )	void f3 ( )
{	{	{
f1( );	f3 ( );	some code
f2 ( );	}	}
}	void f2 ( )	
	{	
	some code	
	}	

including the prototype into funs2.c is important!

Even though function f3 does not call f1 or f2, the compiler will see the prototype for function f3. The compiler will verify that the prototype matches the actual code for the function

f3. If f3 were not coded with the correct number and type of parameters, or with the wrong return type (versus the prototype) the compiler would issue a warning.

This is yet another check that our promised interface (prototype) matches the actual code

we wrote and also how we will use it.

prog35.c multiple files being compiled together

```
/* main routine located in one file * /
/* subrl is located in another file func35a.c */
/* subr2 is located in another file func35b.c */
/* compile together via
        acc -o prog35 prog35.c func35a.c func35b.c
*/
/* try acc prog35.c
   then try acc prog35.c func35a.c
   then try ace func35a.c func35b.c
        then try ace -c prog35.c
*/
/* this is where program execution starts */
main ( )
 {
        /* declaring that main will call subrlO */
        void subr1(int);
        void subr2(int);
        printf("In main routine \n");
        subr1(5);
        printf("Main routine location 1\n\n");
        subr2(3);
        printf("Main routine location 2\n\n");

 }
```

func35a.c

/* program execution does not start here */

/* this code is only executed when the subrl routine is called */

void subr1(int n)

```c
{
        void subr2(int);
        /* n is an argument passed from main routine * /
        /* i is a local argument, it will live on stack */
        /* it will be deallocated when routine exits */
        int i;
        for ( i = 0; i  < n; i++ )
        {
                printf("In subrl\n");
                subr2( -17);
                return;
        }
}
```

func35b.c

/* program execution does not start here * /

/* this code is only executed when the subrl routine is called */

void subr2(int n)

```c
{
        /* n is an argument passed from main routine * /
        /* i is a local argument, it will live on stack */
        /* it will be deallocated when routine exits */
        printf("In subr2\n");
        printf("Square of %i is %i \n",n, n*n);
        return;
}
```

valref.c Call By Value vs. Call by Reference

```c
/* demonstrate call by value and call by reference */
void val1(int x)                    /* ansi function header */
{
        x++;                        /* add one to x */
        printf("In val1 x = %i \n",x); /* print out its value */
        return;                     /* return to calling routine */
}


void ref1 (int* x)      /* ansi function header */
{
        *x = *x + 1;    /* add one to value stored at address stored in x */
        printf("In ref1 x = %i \n",*x);/* print it out */
        return;
}
main( )
{
        int i = 5;

        printf("In main i = %i \n",i);
        val1 (i);                   /* pass value of i to val1 */
        printf("In main i = %i \n",i); /* notice that val1 did not change i */

        printf("In main i = %i \n",i);
        ref1(&i);                   /* pass address of i to ref1 */
        printf("In main i = %i \n",i); /* notice that ref1 changed i */
}
In main i = 5
In val1 x = 6
In main i = 5
In main i = 5
In ref11x = 6
In main i = 6
```

call by value

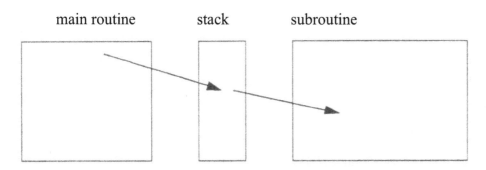

main routine   stack   subroutine

values are placed on stack

subroutine cannot "see" memory of main routine

subroutine can only "see" values on stack

call by reference

addresses are placed on stack

subroutine can "see" memory of main routine through addresses found on stack

Exercise 11

/* PART ONE */

/* write a program to input a number */

/*

        Print the number in the main routine.

        Pass the number to a subroutine by value.

        Have the subroutine print the received value

        Have the subroutine return twice the input value.

        Have the main routine print the original and the result.

*/

/* PART TWO */

/* write a program to input a number */

/*

        Pass the number to a subroutine by reference.

        Have the subroutine multiply the value by three.

        Have the main routine print the original value and the result.

*/

Solution for Exercise 11

```
main( )
{
            int i;
            intj;
            int twice(int);
            void three_times(int *);

            printf("Enter number \n");
            scanf("%i",&i);
            printf("You entered %i \n",i);

            j = twice(i);
            printf("Twice %i is %i\n",i,j);

            printf("three times %i is ",i);
            three_times(&i);
            printf("%i \n",i);
}


int twice( int n )
{
        return (n * 2 );
}


void three_times( int * nptr )
{
        *nptr *= 3;
        return;
}
```

prog36.c

```c
main ( )
{
        /* scores[0] is the zeroeth entry in scores */
        /* &scores[0] is the address of the zeroeth entry */
        /* scores all by itself, is semantically equivalent to &scores[0] */
        int scores[5], i;
        int determine 1 ( int values[5] );
        int determine2( int * );

        /* useful to use data file prog36.dat */
        printf("Please enter five scores \n");
        for ( i = 0; i < 5; i++ )
        {
                printf("Score %i: ",i);
                scanf("%i",&scores[i]);
                printf("\t %i \n",scores[i])

                if ( determine1 (scores) == 1 )
                        printf("23 was in array \n");
                else
                        printf("23 was not in array \n");

                if ( determine2(scores) == 1 )
                        printf("50 was in array \n");
                else
                        printf("50 was not in array \n");

                if ( determine3(scores) == 1)
                        printf("50 was in array \n");
                else
                        printf("50 was not in array \n");
```

```
        }
}
```

prog36.c   passing arrays to subroutines

```
/* write functions to find out if a value is in an array */
#define        SUCCESS    1
#define        FAILURE    2
/* function returns an integer */
/* function name is determine */
/* function accepts array of ten integers */
/* what it is really accepting is a pointer to the first element of the array */
int determine1 ( int values[5] ) {
        int i;
        for ( i  = 0; i < 5; i++ ) {
                if ( values[i] == 23 )
                        return(SUCCESS);
        }
        return(FAILURE;


int determine2 ( int * x) {
int i;
        for ( i  = 0; i  < 5; i++ ) {
                if ( x[i] == 50 )
                        return(SUCCESS );
        }
        return(FAILURE);
}
int determine3 ( int* x ) {
        int i;
        for (i = 0; i < 5; i++ ) {
                if ( *(x+i) == 50 )
                        return(SUCCESS);
        }
```

```
        return(FAILURE);
}
```

prog37.c passing pointers and arrays to subroutines

```c
/* function to subtract every element by the element after it* /
/* leave the last element alone */
/* this function demonstrates that array elements can be */
/* manipulated by the function */
/* arrayptr is a pointer to an integer */
/* IT HAPPENS TO BE THE FIRST ELEMENT OF A TEN ELEMENT ARRAY */
void subtracts( int • array _ptr )
{
        int i;
        for (i = 0; i < 9; i++ )
                array _ptr[i] = array _ptr[i] - array _ptr[i+ 1];
}

main ( )
{
        int scores[10], i;
        void subtracts( int * );

        /* useful to use data file prog36.dat */
        printf("Please enter ten scores \n");
        for ( i = 0; i < 10; i++ )
        {
                printf("Score %i: ",i);
                scanf("%i",&scores[i]);
                printf("\t %i \n",scores[i]);
        }
        printf("Array before function call \n");
        for ( i = 0; i < 10; i++ )
                printf("scores[%i]\t%i\n",i,scores[i]);

        subtracts( scores );
        printf("Array after function call \n");
        for ( i = 0; i < 10; i++ )
                printf("scores [%i]\t%i\n",i,scores [i]);
}
```

prog38.c   sorting an array of integers

```c
/* function to sort an array of integers into ascending order */

/* problem is, we can't hard code the size of the array into the function */

/* first solution is to pass the size of the array into function */

/* function returns nothing */

/* its name is sort * /

/* it expects an integer array, doesn't know how big it will be yet */

/* n will be an integer specifying the size of the array */

void sort ( int *a, int n)

{

        int i,j,temp;
        for ( i = 0; i < n -1; i++ )

        {

                for (j = i + 1; j < n; j++ )

                {

                        if ( a[i] > a[j] )

                        {

                                temp = a[i];
                                a[i] = a[j];
                                a[j] = temp;

                        } /* end if */

                } /* end for j loop */

        } /* end for i loop */

} /* end sort function */


#define  MAX_ARRAY  100

/* main routine to call sort and display results */

main ( )

{

        int i;
        int num_elements;
        /* don't know how big array needs to be */
        int array[MAX_ARRAY] ;
```

```c
void sort( int *, int);
/* get and error check number of elements */
printf("How many elements in array'!\n");
scanf("%i" ,&num_elements);
if (num_elements < 0 || num_elements > MAX_ARRAY)
{
        printf("Impossible number of elements\n");
        exit(-1);
}
/* have a good number of elements, continue */
for ( i = 0; i < num_elements; i++ )
 {
        printf("Enter value for element %i \n",i);
        scanf(" %i ",&array[i]);
}
printf("The array before the sort is:\n");
for ( i = 0; i < num_elements; i++ )
        printf("%i ",array [i]);
printf("\n\n");

/* call the subroutine to do the sort */
/* pass the address of the array and number of elements */
sort(array, num_elements);

printf("The array after the sort is: \n");
for ( i = 0; i < num_elements; i++ )
printf("%i ",array[i]);
printf("\n\n") ;

}
```

How many elements in array?

5

Enter value for element 0

1

Enter value for element 1

4

Enter value for element 2

2

Enter value for element 3

3

Enter value for element 4

9

The array before the sort is:

1 4 2 3 9

The array after the sort is:

1 2 3 4 9

sortstep.c

```c
void sortstep(int *, int, int);
main ( )
{
        int i,j;
        int array[3][4] =
        {
                { 0, 1,2,3 },
                { -1, -2, -3, -4 },
                { 10, 20, 30, 40 }
        };

        printf("array before call is \n");
        for ( i = 0; i < 3; i++ )
        {
                for (j = 0; j < 4; j++ )
                        printf("%3i ",array[i][j]);
                printf("\n");
        }
        sortstep (&array [0] [0],3,4);
        printf("array after call is \n");
        for ( i = 0; i < 3; i++ ) {
                for ( j = 0; j < 4; j++ )
                printf("%3i ",array[i] [j]);
                printf("\n");
        }
        sortstep(&array[1] [0],4, 1);
        printf("array after call is \n");
        for ( i = 0; i < 3; i++ )
        {
                for (j = 0; j < 4; j++ )
                        printf("%3i ",array[i][j]);
```

```c
                printf("\n");
        }
}

void sortstep ( int *a, int n, int stepsize)
{
        int i, j, temp;
        int iindex, jindex;
        for ( i = 0; i < n -1; i++ )
        {
                iindex = i * stepsize;
                for (j = i + 1; j < n; j++ )
                {
                        jindex = j * stepsize;
                        if ( a[iindex] > a[ jindex ] )
                        {
                                temp = a[iindex];
                                a[iindex] = ajjindex];
                                aljindex] = temp;
                        } /* end if */
                } /* end for j  loop */
        } /* end for i loop */
} /* end sort function */

array before call is
0 1 2 3
-1 -2 -3 -4
10 20 30 40

array after call is
-1 1 2 3
0 -2 -3 -4
 10 20 30 40

array after call is
-1 1 2 3
 -4 -3 -2 0
 10 20 30 40
```

prog39.c program to introduce two dimensional arrays

```c
main( )
{
        /* rc cola */
        /* rows, columns */
        /* 2 rows, three columns */
/* C THINKS OF SAMPLE_MATRIX AS AN ARRAY WITH TWO ENTRIES EACH
                ENTRY HAPPENS TO BE AN ARRAY OF THREE ENTRIES */
        /* sample_matrix[0] is an array, sample_matrix[0][0] is an integer */
        int sample_matrix[2] [3] =
                {
                        { 1,2,3 },
                        { 3,5,9 }
                } ;
        int row,column;
        int rowsum, colsum;

        /* print original matrix */
        printf("Original matrix \n");
        for ( row = 0; row < 2; row++)
        {
                for (column = 0; column < 3; column++ )
                                printf("%3i" ,sample_matrix[row][column]);
                printf("\n") ;
        }
        printf("\n\nMATRIX WITH ROWSUMS AND COLUMN SUMS\n");
        /* add up rows and columns, produce report */
        printf("\t\t rowsum\n");
        for ( row = 0; row < 2; row ++ )
        {
                rowsum =0;
                printf("\t");
                for ( column = 0; column < 3; column++ )
                {
                        printf("%3i" ,sample_matrix [row ] [column]);
                        rowsum += sample_matrix[row][column];
                }
                printf(" %4i\n",rowsum);
        }
        printf("\n");
        printf("colsum\t");

        for ( column = 0; column < 3; column++ )

        {

                colsum = 0;

                for ( row = 0; row < 2; row++ )
```

```
                colsum += sample_matrix[row] [column];
            printf("%3i" ,colsum);
        }
        printf('\n\n');
}


/* sample output */
/*
Original matrix
  1 2 3
  3 5 9
MATRIX WITH ROWSUMS AND COLUMN SUMS
                rowsum
        1 2 3   6
        3 5 9   17
colsum    4 7 12
*/
```

Sending Two Dimensional Array To Subroutine

twodim.c

```c
main( )
{
/* function prototype header must supply row and column information
                if we wish to use multiple sets of [] in subroutine */
        void s1( int a[2][3] );
        /* x all by itself is the address of the 1st array * /
        int x[2][3] =    /* x is an array with two elements, each element is itself an array */
        {
                {1,2,3},
                { 4,5,6}
        };
        printf(" AA \n");
        s1(x);  /* call using just name of array, resolves to &x[0], an array */

        printf("BB\n");
        sl(&x[0]);  /* call using address of first "array of arrays */

        printf("CC\n");
        sl(&x[0][0]);  /* call using address of first element of first array*
                        /* compiler warning b/c this is address of an integer, not an array
*/
}

void s1(int x[2][3] )
/* converted to int**    */
{
        int i,j;
        for ( i = 0; i < 2; i++ )
        {
                for (j = 0; j < 3;
                j++ )
                {
                        /* function declaration informs us of how many rows and
                        columns */
                        printf("%i ",x[i] U] );
                }
                printf(
                "\n");

        }
}
```

Solution for Exercise 13

```
/* function returns nothing */
/* its name is sort */
/* it expects an integer array, doesn't know how big it will be yet */

/* n will be an integer specifying the size of the array */

void sort ( int a[ ], int n)

{

        int i,j,temp;
        for (i = 0; i < n; i++ )

        {

                for (j = i  + 1; j < n; j++ )

                {

                        if ( a[i] > a[j] )

                        {

                                temp = a[i];
                                a[i] = a[j];
                                a[j] = temp;

                        } /* end if */

                } /* end for j loop *

        } /* end for i loop */

} /* end sort function *
```

```
#define ROWS      3
#define COLS      4
main( )
{
        int input_array[ROWS][COLS];
        int temp_array[ROWS][COLS];
        int final_array[ROWS][COLS];
        int row[COLS], col[ROWS];
        void sort ( int a[ ], int n );
        int i,j;
        /* get and print original array */
        printf("\n");
        for (i  =0; i < ROWS; i++ )
        {
                for (j = 0; j < COLS; j++)
                {
                        scanf("%i",&input_array[i][j]);
                        printf("%3i",input_array[i][j]));
                }
                printf("\n");
        }

        for ( i =0; i < ROWS; i++ )    /* sort by row */
        {
                for (j = 0; j < COLS; j++)
                        row[j] = input_array[i][j]:
                sort(row,COLS);
                for (j = 0; j < COLS; j++ )
                        temp_array[i][j] = row[j];
        }
        printf('\n\nAFfER SORTING ROWS\n"); /* print array */
        for ( i = 0; i < ROWS; i++ )
        {
```

```c
        for (j = 0; j < COLS; j++ )
                printf("%3i" ,temp _array[i]
        u]);
        printf("\n");
    }
    for (j = 0; j < COLS; j++ ) /* sort by column */
    {
        for ( i = 0; i < ROWS; i++ )
                col[i] = temp_array[i][j];
        sort(col,ROWS);
        for ( i = 0; i < ROWS; i++ )
                final_array[i][j] = col[i];
    }
    printf("\n\nAFTER SORTING COLS\n"); /* print array */
    for ( i  = 0; i  < ROWS; i++ )
    {
        for (j = 0; j < COLS; j++ )
                printf("%3i" ,final_array[i][j]):
        printf("\n"):
    }
    printf("\n");
} /* end main */
```

sample output
```
 1 3 2 15
 3 8 0 2
 9 4 -3 12
AFTER SORTING ROWS
  1 2 3 15
 0 2 3 8
 -3 4 9 12
AFTER SORTING COLS
 -3 2 3 8
  0 2 3 12
  1 4 9 15
```

More Array Syntax & Subroutines

testarrays.c

The basic problem when communicating array information to a subroutine is how many rows
and how many columns, (or how many entries per dimension) the array has. Basic pointer syntax only provides the address of the first element. This is fine if we wish to only traverse the
memory allocated for the array, however, if we wish to traverse it using the row and column layout we have specified when the array was created, we need to provide some row column information to the subroutine. As a rule, if there are N dimensions in the array you need to provide at least N-1 pieces of dimension information, the computer can figure out the last dimension. However, to be rigorous, why not provide as much as possible, all N if you know it. There are applications when you won't know the last dimension information.

```c
void s1(int *
x,int n)
{
        int i;
        for ( i = 0; i < n; i++ )
                printf("%5i", x[i]);
        printf("\n");
}


void
s2(int
x)
{
        printf("0x%x",x);
        printf("\n");
}
```

```
main ( )
{
        void sl(int *,int );
        void s2(int);
        int one[5];
        int two[3][4]; two[0][0] = 0;
         two[0][1]  = 1
        two[0][2] = 2;
         two[0][3] = 3;


        two[1][0] = 10;
        two[1][1] = 11;
        two[1][2] = 12;
        two[1][3] = 13;


        two[2][0] = 100;
        two[2][1] = 101;
        two[2][2] = 102;
        two[2][3] = 103;


        one[0] = 0;
        one[l] = 1;
        one[2] = 2;
        one[3] = 3;


        printf("FIRST PRINT\n");
        sl(one,S);              /* array name by itself is pointer */
        sl(&one[2],3);          /* subscripted element needs & */
        s1(one + 2,3);          /* subscripted element needs & */


#if 0
        sl(one[2],3);   /* this would be run time error, subscripted element needs & */
#endif
```

```c
    s2(one);   /* array name by itself is pointer, routine expecting int, prints it as int */
    s2(one[3]);      /* subscripted element is a value, routine expecting value, okay */
    printf("SECOND PRINT\n");
    sl(two,12); /* name of array by itself is pointer */
    sl(two[0],4); /* name of array by itself is pointer, two[0] is name of an array
            because two is an array of three elements,
            of which each element is itself an array */
    sl(two[1],4); /* name of array by itself is pointer */
    sl(two[2],4); /* name of array by itself is pointer */


#if 0
    sl(two[0][0],12);      /* subscripted element is value,
                            routine expecting address, core dump
*/
#endif
    sl(&two[0][0],12);              /* subscripted element needs & */
    s2(two);
    s2(two[0]);
    s2(two[1]);
    s2(two[2]);
    s2( two [0] [0]);
    s2(two[1][0]);
    s2(two[2][0]);
    s2(&two[0]);
```

SAMPLE OUTPUT

FIRST PRINT

0 1 2 3 4

2 3 4

Oxf7fffb34

Ox3

SECOND PRINT

0 1 2 3 10 11 12 13 100 101 102 103

0 1 2 3

10 11 12 13

100 101 102 103

0 1 2 3 10 11 12 13 100 101 102 103

Oxf7fffb04

Oxf7fffb04

Oxf7fffb14

Oxf7fffb24

OxO

Oxa

Ox64

0xf7fffb04

Yet Even More Array Syntax & Subroutines

test_arrays1.c

```c
void s 1 (int * x,int n)
{
        /* will access as many as you say starting where you say */
        int i;
      for ( i =0; i < n; i++ )
        printf("%5i" ,x[i]);
      printf("\n");
}


void s2(int * x, int rows, int cols)
{
        /* wants to use multiple square brackets, needs dimension info */
        int i,j;
        for ( i = 0; i < rows; i++ )
        {
                for ( j = 0; j < cols; j++ )
                {
#if 0
                        /* this will be a compiler error */
                        /* routine does not have info on row,column
                        layout of memory associated with x */
                        printf("%4i ",x [i][j]);
#endif
                }
        }
}
```

```
void s3(int x[3][4],int rows,int cols )
{
        /* wants to use multiple square brackets, needs dimension info */
        int i,j;
        for ( i = 0; i < rows; i++ )
        {
                for (j = 0; j < cols; j++ )
                {
                        /* this will be a compiler error */
                        /* routine does not have info on row,column
                        layout of memory associated with x */
                        printf("%4i ",x[i] [j]);
                }
        }
}
```

```
main ( )
{
        void s 1 (int * ,int );
        void s2(int * ,int,int );
        void s3(int [3][4],int,int);

        int one[5];
        int two[3][4];
        two[0][0] = 0; two[0][1] = 1;
        two[0][2] = 2; two[0][3] = 3;
        two[1][0] = 10; two[1][1] = 11;
        two[1][2] = 12; two[1][3] = 13;
        two[2][0] = 100; two[2][1] = 101;
        two[2][2] = 102; two[2][3] = 103;
        one[0] = 0; one[1] = 1; one[2] = 2;
        one[3] = 3; one[ 4] = 4;

        /* call s 1 sending different lengths */
        printf("\ncalling s 1 \n");
        s1(one,5);
        s1(two,12);  /* will be compiler warning */
        s 1 (one, 10);

        /* try to call s2 , it won't work */
        printf("\ncalling s2 \n");
        s2(one,1,5);
        s2(two,3,4); /* will be compiler warning */
        /* try to call s3 * /

        printf("\ncalling s3 for one\n");
        s3(one,1,5);/* will be compiler warning */
        printf("\ncalling s3 for two \n");
        s3(two,3,4);
        printf("\ncalling s3 for one\n");
        s3(one,2,4);/* will be compiler warning */
        printf("\n");

}
```

acc testarrays 1.c

"testarrays 1.c", line 70: warning: argument is incompatible with prototype: arg #1

"testarrays1.c", line 76: warning: argument is incompatible with prototype: arg #1

"testarrays1.c", line 80: warning: argument is incompatible with prototype: arg #1

"testarraysl.c", line 84: warning: argument is incompatible with prototype: arg #1

a.out

calling sl

0 1 2 3 4

0 1 2 3 10 11 12 13 100 101 102 103

0 1 2 3 4 0 0 0 0 0

calling s2

calling s3 for one

0 1 2 3 4

calling s3 for two

0 1 2 3 10 11 12 13 100 10 1 102 103

calling s3 for one

0 1 2 3 4 0 0 0

prog40.c static, automatic, global keywords

```
/* two possible compile strings

        acc -D COMPVAR1 prog40.c additional code

        acc prog40.c            no additional code */


/* program to demonstrate static and automatic variables */

/* program to demonstrate global variables */

/* we already did this once, do it again */

/* automatic variables go on the stack */

/* static variables go in data area */

int g; /* no initial value is assigned */


void subrl ( void)
{

        int local_ variable_is_auto = 1;

        static int local_ variable_is_static = 1;

        local_variable_is_auto++;

        local_ variable_is_static++;

        g++;

        printf("%i %i %i\n", local_ variable_is_auto, local_ variable_is_static,g);

}


main ( )
{
        void subr1 (void);
        g = 0;
        printf("Global variable = %i \n",g);
        subr1( );
        g++;
        subr1( );
#ifdef COMPVAR1
        local_ variable_is_auto++;
        local_ variable_is_static++;
        printf("%i %i %i\n", local_ variable_is_auto, local_ variable_is_static,g);
        printf("%i\n",g);
#endif
}
```

Scope.c   Scope of Variables

```c
int i = 1;          /* global variable */
void subr1(void);
void subr2(void);
main ( )
{
        /* local i overrides global i */
        int i  = 2;
        printf("AAA i = %i \n",i);

        /* call subroutine to test scope */
        subr1( );
        {
                int i  = -8032;
                printf("\tBBB i = %i \n",i);
        }

        /* call subroutine to test scope */
        subr2( );
}


void subr1( )
{
        /* local i overrides global i */
        int i = 23;
        printf("\tCCC( i = %i \n", i);
        {
                /* interior i overrides exterior i */
                int i = -98;
                printf("\t\tDDD i = %i \n",i);
        }
}


void subr2( )
{
        /* no local i, refers to global i */
        printf("\t\t\tEEE i = %i \n",i);
        {
                /* no local i, refers to global i */
                printf("\t\t\t\tFFF i = %i \n",i);
        }
}
```

AAAi=2

CCCi = 23

DDD i = -98

BBB i = -8032

EEEi = 1

FFFi= 1

Definition: recursive *adj.* see recursive[1]

prog41.c Recursion

/* program illustrating recursive function */

/* recursive
function */
```c
int length(char *
s)
{
        printf("In length\n");
        if ( *s == '\0')
                return(1);
        else
                return(1 + length(s + 1) );
}


main ( )
{
        char string[20];
        printf("Enter a
string \n");
        scanf("%s"
,&string);
        printf("You entered %s\n",string);
        printf("Its length is %i \n", length(string) );
}
```

Recursion can be misused. This is actually a poor example of 'tail recursion' (when the last thing
a routine does is call itself). Most tail-recursive programs are better written iteratively including
this one. Recursion is best used when the problem itself can be described in it's simpliest
terms in a recursive manner (splitting a string in half, and in half etc), or the data structures

involved may be viewed as recursive (binary trees, fractals)[2].

1. definition found in several sources, not possible to identify first author

2. See the book *Data Structures and Program Design in* C, for a good reference on recursion in C and guidelines on when to and not to use it. This book also contains a section in one appendix on removing recursion from programs.

testpop.c

```
/* if you implemented s 1 here, there would be compiler errors
when you tried to send a different argument list */
main ( )
{
/* if you had a prototype, you would get compiler errors
                    when you tried to send a different argument list */
        s1( );
        s1(l0);
        s1(100,200);
        s1 (1000,2000,3000);
        s1 (10000,20000,30000,40000);
}
/* you need to declare it int to avoid redefining the default argument type */
int s1(int a, int b)
{
        printf("a is %i \n",a);
        printf("b is %i \n",b);
        printf("\n");
}


a is 0
b is 124
a is 10
b is 124
a is 100
b is 200
a is 1000
b is 2000
a is 10000
b is 20000
```

Exercise 14

/* write a program with functions to do array math */

/* use the two arrays */

/* array! = { 1,2,3,4} */

/* array2 = {5, 6, 7, 8} */

/* have a fuction to add the two arrays */

/* { 6, 8, 10, 12 }   */

/* have a function to multiply the arrays */

/* { 5, 12, 21, 32 }   */

/* have a funtion to do the mproduct of the arrays */

/* { (1 *5 + 1 *6 + 1 *7 + 1 *8)

   (2*5 + 2*6 + 2*7 + 2*8)

   (3*5 + 3*6 + 3*7 + 3*8)

   (4*5 + 4*6 + 4*7 + 4*8) } */

/* allow the user to specify which function they want */

/* to perform, have them type q to quit */

/* allow them to enter functions until they decide to quit */

Solution for Exercise 14

```c
void add_arrays ( int a[], int b[ ], int size)
{
        int, temp;
        printf("Add arrays \n");
        printf("Array1\tArray2\t:Sum\n");
        for ( i = 0; i < size; i++ )
        {
                temp = a[i] + b[i];
                printf("%i\t%i\t%i \n" ,a[i] ,b[i] ,temp );
        }
        return;
}

void mult_arrays (int a[], int b[] , int size)
{
        int i, temp;
        printf("Multiply arrays \n");
        printf("Array1\tArray2\tMult\n");
        for ( i = 0; i < size; i++ )
        {
                temp = a[i] * b[i];
                printf("%i\t%i\t%i \n",a[i] ,b[i] ,temp );
        }
        return;
}

void product arrays (int a[], int b[] , int size)
{
        int i,j,temp;
        printf("product arrays \n");
        printf("M Product\n");
        for ( i = 0; i < size; i++ )
        {
                temp = 0;
                for (j = 0; j < size; j++ )
                {
                        temp = temp + a[i] * b[j];
                printf("%i\n" ,temp);
                }
        return;
 }
```

```c
main ( )
{
        void add_arrays (int a[ ], int b[ ] , int size);
        void mult_arrays (int a[ ], int b[ ] , int size);
        void product arrays (int a[ ], int b[ ] , int size);
        int a1 [ ] = { 1, 2, 3, 4 }; int a2[ ] = { 5, 6, 7, 8 };
        char choice, carriage_return;
        choice = ' ';
        while ( choice != 'q' )
         {
                printf("\nEnter choice:\n");
                printf("a add\n");
                printf("m multiply\n");
                printf("p product\n");
                printf("q quit\n");

                scanf(" %c",&choice);
                printf("You entered %c\n",choice);
                scanf("%c", &carriage_return);
                switch ( choice)
                {
                        case 'a':
                                add_arrays(a1 ,a2,4);
                                break;
                        case'm':
                                multarrays(a1,a2,4);
                                break;
                        case 'p':
                                product_arrays(a1,a2,4);
                                break;
                        case 'q':
                                break;
                        default:
                                printf("\alnvalid input\n");
                                break;
                } /* end switch */
        } /* end while */
} /* end main */
```

exseven.c

```c
void add_arrays( int * a, int * b, int size)
{
            inti, temp;
            for ( i = 0; i < size; i++ )
            {
                        temp = a[i] + b[i];
            }
             return;
}
```

prog42.c simple stucture (struct keyword)

```c
main ( )
{
        /* syntax is: data type then name of variable */
        int     i;
        float   f1;


        /* syntax is: struct then name of structure type */
        /* this is a definition of a type, not a declaration of a vraiable of that type */
        struct date
        {
                /* elements of structure declared like variables */
                int month;
                int day;
                int year;
        };
        /* syntax is: data type then name of variable */
        struct date x;  ◄──────────────── x is the name of the variable to be created
```

struct indicates

that next word

is user defined data type

date is the user defined data type

```c
        x.month = 4;
        x.day = 28;
        x.year = 1992;
        printf("Today's date is %i/%i/%i. \n", x.month,x.day,x.year);
}
```
sample output

Today's date is 4/28/1992.

prog43.c structures with heterogenous components

/* program for debt_trade manipulation */

/* let's assume that debts cannot be traded on certain days, i.e. Christmas */

```c
main ( )
{
        struct debttrade
        {
                int day;
                int month;
                int year;
                float price;
                float par;
        } ;
        struct debt trade        d1;

        struct debt_trade        d2;


        printf("Enter info for first debt trade \n");

        printf("day month year \n");

        scanf("%i %i %i",&d1.day, &dl.month, &d1.year);

        printf("price par \n");

        scanf("%f %f",&d1.price,&d1.par);


        printf("Enter info for second debt trade \n");

        printf("day month year \n");

        scanf("%i %i %i",&d2.day, &d2.month, &d2.year);

        printf("price par \n");

        scanf("%f %f",&d2.price,&d 1.par);


        if ( d1.day ==25 && d1.month == 12 )

                printf("Cannot trade d1 on requested day \n");

        if (d2.day == 25 && d2.month == 12)

                printf("Cannot trade d2 on requested day \n");

}
```

Exercise 15

/* write a c program that has a structure to keep track

      of what time it is now. Structure should be

      able to store current hour, minutes, seconds

      Display the current time and what time it would be after one second.

      Continue to read in times until the time read in is -1 -1 -1

*/

Solution for Exercise 15

```
/* program to illustrate structures some more */
struct time
{
        int     hour;
        int     minutes;
        int     seconds;
};


main( )
{
        struct time time_update ( struct time );
        struct time current time;
        struct time next time;
}

        printf("Enter the time (hh:mm:ss): ");
        scanf("%i: %i: %i",&current_time.hour,
        &current_time.minutes,&current_time.seconds);

        /* loop until sentinel record is found */
        while (current_time.hour != -1 && current jime.minutes !=-1
                && current_time. seconds != -1 )
        {
```

```c
        printf("You entered %.2i:%.2i:%.2i\n",current_time.hour,
        current_time. minutes , current_time.seconds);
        next_time = time_update ( current_time );
        printf("Update time is %.2i:%.2i:%.2i\n", next_time.hour,
        next_time.minutes, next_time.seconds):
        printf("Enter the time (hh:mm:ss): ");
        scanf("%i:%i:%i", &current_time.hour,
                &current_time.minutes, &current_time.seconds);
}
/* function to update the time by one second */
struct time time_update ( struct time now)
{
        now.seconds++;
        if ( now.seconds ==  60 )
        {
                now. seconds = 0;
                now.minutes++;
                if ( now. minutes == 60 )
                {
                        now.minutes = 0;
                        now.hour++;
                        if ( now. hour == 24 )
                        {
                                now. hour = 0;
                        }
                }
        }
        return(now);
}
```

prog45.c   UNIX time.h file

```
/* program illustrates use of include file and predefined structures in time.h */
/* introduces concept of pointer to a structure */
#include <time.h>
main ( )
{
        long timeval;

        /* a variable that points to a structure of type tm */
        struct tm * tp;

        /* a function, local time, that returns a pointer to a structure of type tm */
        struct tm * localtime( );

        /* a function, ctime, that returns a pointer to a character */
        extern char * ctime( );

        /* get time from UNIX system */
        /* time is a system call returns the number of
                clock ticks since midnight, new year's eve, 1970 */
        time ( &timeval );
        /* ctime takes the tick count and produces a string of characters that can be
        displayed with %s format */
        printf("GMT time is %s \n", ctime( & timeval ) );

        /* get tm structure */
        /* locatime accepts the tick count and returns a pointer to a structure that it filled
        up with values that it derived out of the tick count */
        tp = localtime(&timeval);

        /* tp is a pointer to a structure * /
        printf("Structure members are:\n");
```

```
    printf("Seconds        %d\n",tp->tm_sec);
    printf("Minutes        %d\n",tp->tm_min);
    printf("Hours  %d\n",tp->tm_hour);
    printf("Day of Month  %d\n",tp->tm_mday);
    printf("Month of Year %d\n",tp->tm_mon); r zero based off by one */
    printf("Year           %d\n",tp->tm_year); /* 2 digit year obsolete in 2000... */
    printf("Weekday        %d\n",tp->tm_wday);
    printf("Day of Year    %d\n",tp->tm-yday);
    printf("Daylight Savings? %d\n",tp->tm_isdst);
}
```

GMT time is Thu Jun 4 15:59:21 1992

Structure members are:

Seconds   21

Minutes   59

Hours   15

Day of Month   4

Month of Year   5

Year   92

Weekday   4

Day of Year   155

Daylight Savings? 1

Note: the month number is zero based (Jan=O, Dece1 1).

Why do you think it is this way?

prog46.c   Arrays of Structures

```c
/* program to illustrate arrays of structures */
#define          NUM_RECS 7
struct xyz { int h; int m; int s; };
main( )
{
        struct xyz   next second ( struct xyz now);
        struct xyz   array_structs[NUM_RECS] =
        {        {11,59,59},
                 { 12, 0, 0 },
                 { -1, -4, -30 },
                 { 1, 1, 60 },
                 { 1,29,59},
                 { 23,59, 59 },
                 {19,12,27}      };


        int i;
        struct xyz t1 ,t2;
        printf("\nT1 %i %i %i\n", arrayof structsl[1].h, array ofstructs[1].m,
                array _of_structs[ 1].s);

        array_of_structs[ 1] = next_second ( array of' structs[1] );
        printf("T2 %i %i %i\n",array_of_structs[1].h,
                array_of_structs[1].m, array_of_structs[1].s);
        for (i = 0; i < NUM_RECS; i++)
        {
                printf("\nT1 %i %i %i\n", arrayof structs[i].h, arrayof structs[i].m,
                 array _of_structs[i].s);
                t1 = array_of_structs[i];/* memberwise copy of data */

                /* validate the data */
                if ( t1.h >= 0 && t1.h <= 23 && t1.m >= 0 && t1.m <= 59 &&
```

```
                    t1.s >= 0 && tl.s <= 59)

                 t2 = next second ( t1 );

                 printf("Time one second later is %i %i %i\n", t2.h, t2.m, t2.s);

             else

                 printf("INVALID DATA \n");

        }

   }
```

```c
/* function to update the xyz by one second */
struct xyz next_second ( struct xyz now)
{
        now.s++;
        switch (now.s)
        {
                case 60:
                        now.s = 0;
                        now.m++;
                        switch(now.m)
                        {
                                case 60:
                                        now.m =0;
                                        now.h++;
                                        switch(now.h)
                                        {
                                                case 24:
                                                        printf("The Start Of A New Day \n");
                                                        now.h =0;
                                                        break;
                                                default:
                                                        return(now);
                                        }
                                        break;
                                default:
                                        return(now);
                        }
                        break;
                default:
                        return(now);
        }
        return(now); }
```

prog47.c Structures and Arrays

```c
/* shows an array of characters inside a structure defined two ways */
struct piece
{
        int     point_value;
        char name[8];
};
/* global data structure po nested curly braces to initialize sub-structures*/
struct piece po[ ] =
        {
                { 20, "KING" },
                { 10, "QUEEN" },
                { O5, "BISHOP" },
                { 04, "KNIGHT" },
                { 07, "ROOK" },
                { 01, "PAWN" }      };

main ( )
{
        int i;
        /* local data structure */
        struct piece pi[ 6] =
        {       { 20, { 'K', 'i', 'n', 'g', ' ' , } },
                { 10, { 'Q', 'u', 'e', 'e', 'n' } },
                { 05, { 'B', 'i', 's', 'h', 'o', 'p' } },
                {04, { 'K', 'n', 'i', 'g', 'h', 't' } },
                { 07, { 'R', 'o', 'o', 'k', ' ' , } },
                { 01, { 'P', 'a', 'w', 'n', ' ' , } }
        } ;

        printf("Piece\t Val ue\n");
        printtf("-----\t-----\n"):
        for ( i = 0; i < 6; i++ )
```

```
        {
                printf(" %c%c%c%c%c%c\t%3i\n", pi[i].name[0],
                        pi[i].name[1],pi[i].name[2], pi[i].name[3], pi[i].name[4],
                        pi[i].name[5], pi[i].point_value);
        printf("\n from po \n");
        printf("Piece\tValue\n");
        printff("------\t------\n");
        for ( i =0; i < 6; i++ )
                printf("%s\t%3i\n", po[i].name,po[i].point_value);
}
```

Piece	Value
King	20
Queen	10
Bishop	5
Knight	4
Rook	7
Pawn	1

from po

Piece	Value
King	20
Queen	10
Bishop	5
Knight	4
Rook	7
Pawn	1

Exercise 16

write a program that reads in an opening balance

        for a checking account, a list of check numbers

        dates and amounts.

        print out a nice list of the opening balance,

        the list of transactions, sorted by check number

        and the running balance after each transaction

        use structures and functions

sample input data

5000.00

1	1/23/92	25.00
3	1/24/92	23.00
5	2/2/92	127.00
4	2/1/92	93.00
14	4/15/92	4500.00
2	1/23/92	100.00

Sample Output

Opening Balance $5000

Check Number	Transaction Date	Amount	New Balance
1	1/23/92	25.00	4975.00
2	1/23/92	100.00	4875.00
3	1/24/92	23.00	4852.00
4	2/1/92	93.00	4759.00
5	2/2/92	127.00	4632.00

14   4/15/92   4500.00   132.00

Exercise 16.c

```c
#define        MAXRECS 20
struct trans
{
        int chk;
        char date[9];
        float amt;
};
void sorttrans ( tptr, count)
struct trans * tptr;
int count;
{
        int i,j;
        struct trans temp;
        for ( i = 0; i < count - 1; i++ )
        {
                for (j = i + 1; j < count; j++ )
                {
                        if ( tptr[i].chk > tptr[j].chk )
                        {
                                temp = tptr[i];
                                tptrji] = tptr[j];
                                tptr[j] = temp;
                        }
                }
        }
}
```

```
main ( )
{
        struct trans ttrans[MAXRECS];
        void sorttrans( );
        int i,rec,chk;
        float bal,newbal;
        printf("opening balance please \n");
        scanf("%f' ,&bal);

        chk = 0; rec = 0;
        while ( chk != -1 )
        {
                printf("Enter check number \n");
                scanf("%i",&chk);
                if (chk != -1 )
                {
                        ttrans[rec].chk = chk;
                        printf("Enter date mm/dd/yy and amount (float) \n");
                        scanf("%s %f",&ttrans[rec].date,&ttrans[rec].amt);
                        rec++;
        printf("ORIGINAL TABLE \n");
        for ( i = 0;  i  < rec; i++ )
        {
                printf("%i %s %f\n" ,ttrans[i] .chk,ttrans [i] .date,ttrans[i] .amt);
        }

        sorttrans( &ttrans [0] ,rec);
        printf("SORTED TABLE \n");
        for ( i = 0; i < rec; i++ )
        {
                printf("%i %s %f\n", ttrans[i].chk, ttrans[i].date, ttrans[i].amt);
        }

        printf("TABLE with balances \n");
        newbal = bal;
        for ( i = 0; i < rec; i++ )
        {
                newbal = newbal - ttrans[i].amt;
                printf("%i %s %f %t\n",ttrans[i].chk, ttrans[i].date, ttrans[i].amt,newbal);
        }
}
```

exercise16c.dat

```
1000.00
 1
1/1/9350.00
 5
1/2/9325.00
 7
1/3/93 10.00
 2
1/1/9325.00
 3
1/1/9375.00
 8
1/4/93 100.00
 4
1/1/93 5.00
 6
1/2/93 20.00
10
2/28/93100.00
 9
2/15/9330.00
 -1
```

ORIGINAL TABLE

11/1/9350.000000

5 1/2/93 25.000000

7 1!3/93 10.000000

2 1/1/9325.000000

3 1/1/9375.000000

81/4/93 100.000000

4 1/1/93 5.000000

6 1/2/93 20.000000

10 2/28/93 100.000000

9 2/15/,93 30.000000

SORTED TABLE

1 1/1/93 50.000000

2 1/1/93 25.000000

3 1/1/93 75.000000

41/1/935.000000

5 1/2/93 25.000000

6 1/2/93 20.000000

7 1/3/93 10.000000

8 1/4/93 100.000000

9 2/15/93 30.000000

10 2/28/93 100.000000

TABLE with balances
1 1/1/93 50.000000 950.000000
21/1/9325.000000 925.000000
3 1/1/93 75.000000 850.000000
41/1/935.000000 845.000000
5 1/2/93 25.000000 820.000000
6 1/2/93 20.000000 800.000000
7 1/3/93 10.000000 790.000000
8 1/4/93 100.000000 690.000000
9 2/15/93 30.000000 660.000000
10 2/28/93 100.000000 560.000000

prog48.c   String Processing strlen

```
/* function to count the number of characters in a string */
/* also the UNIX function that does the same thing */
#include <string.h>

/* returns a count of how many characters are in string */
/* count does not include null terminator */
/* accepts a null terminated string */
int our_string_length ( char * input string )
{
        int     count = 0;
        /* note the null terminator is binary zero * /
        while (input_string[count] )
                count++;
        return(count);
}

main( )
{
        int our_string_length ( char * string );
        charwordl[ ] = {'T', 'e', 'r', 'r', 'i', 'l', 'l', "\0"};
        char word2[] = { 'O', 'w', 'e', 'n', 's', '\0' };
        printf("USING OUR ROUTINE WE DISCOVER\n");
        printf("length of %s is %i \n",wordl, our_string_length(wordl));
        printf("length of %s is %i \n\n",word2,our_string_length(word2));
        printf("USING BUILT IN ROlITINE WE DISCOVER\n");
        printf("length of %s is %i \n",wordl,strlen(word1));
        printf("length of %s is %i \n",word2,strlen(word2));
}
```


USING OUR ROUTINE WE DISCOVER
length of Terrill is 7
length of Owens is 5
USING BUILT IN ROUTINE WE DISCOVER
length of Terrill is 7
length of Owens is 5

prog49.c   String Processing   strcat

```c
/* program to illustrate string concatenation */
/* uses pointers * /
/* uses built in functions * /
#include <string.h>
#define MAX_SIZE 100
char s1[] = {"Terrill"};
char s2[] = {"Owens"};
char sa[] = {"Oingo " } ;
char sb[] = {"Boingo "};
char s3[MAX_SIZE];
char s4[MAX_SIZE];
char stringa[] = {"abcde "};


/* jtcat concatenates a and b into c, replace c if contains data */
void jtcat( char* a, char* b, char* c)
{
        /* copy all of a into c, stop before copy null terminator */
        while ( *a != '\0' )
        {
                *c++ = *a++;
        }


        /* copy all of b onto end of c * /
        while (*b )
        {
                *c++ = *b++;
        }
        /* remember to tack null terminator onto end of c */
        *c = '\0';
}
```

```
main ( )
{
        void jtcat( char*, char*, char*);        /* jts concatenation routine */


        /* call strcat, send s1 and s2
                        function sticks s2 onto back of s1, returns s1 */
        strcat(s1, s2);
        printf("%s\n",s1);


        /* call strcat, send s3 and s1 */
        /* function sticks s1 onto end of s3, returns s3 */
        strcat(s3,stringa);
        strcat(s3,stringa);
        strcat(s3,stringa);
        strcat(s3,stringa);
        strcat(s3,stringa);
        strcat(s3,stringa);
        printf("%s",s3);
        printf("\n");


        /* now use jtcat routine */
        printf("%s\n",sa);
        printf("%s\n",sb);
        jtcat(sa,sb,s4);
        printf("%s\n\n",s4);
}

        sample output
        Terrill Owens
        abcde abcde abcde abcde abcde abcde
        Oingo
        Boingo
        Oingo Boingo
```

prog50.c   String Processing   strcmp

```c
#include <string.h>
int jteq(char * s1, char * s2)

{

        while (*s1++ == *s2++ )

        {

                if ( *s1 == '\0' && *s2 == '\0')

                        return( 0 ); /* 0 is code for "equal" in my routine */

        }
        return ( 1 );  /* 1 is code for "not equal" in my routine */

}
main ( )

{

        int     jteq( char*, char* );
        char stra[] = "Terrill Owens";
        char strb[] = "Terrill";
        int     equalreturn;
        char * strings[] =
                { "The Same", "Not The Same" };
        int cmp_val1, cmp_val2, cmp_val3;
        equal_return = jteq(stra,stra);
        printf("%s and \n%s are %s \n\n",stra,stra,strings[equal_return]);


        equal_return = jteq(stra,strb);
        printf("%s and \n%s are %s \n\n",stra,strb,strings[equal_return]);
        cmp_val1 = strcmp(stra,stra);
        printf("cmp_val1 => %i \n",cmp_val1);
        cmp_val2 = strcmp(stra,strb);
        printf("cmp_val2 => %i \n",cmp_val2);
        cmp_val3 = strcmp(strb,stra);
        printf("cmp_val3 => %i \n",cmp_val3);

}
```

Exercise 17

Write a program that will input a list of words until the word quit is entered. Create one long string from all these words, seperating them in the created string by a dollar sign. Do not allow the word foobar to be entered into your string. (ignore it if it is entered).

Print out a table which includes each of the words input and its length.

Print out the final created string.

Hint: Use strcat, strlen, and strcmp

Solution For Exercise 17

```c
#include <string.h>
main ( )
{
        int x;
        char s[20];
        char d[ 1000];

        printf("Enter word\n");
        scanf("%s" ,s);
        x = strcmp(s,"quit");
        while ( x != 0 )/* strcmp returns FALSE if a match */
        {
                if ( strcmp(s,"foobar") )
                {
                        strcat(d,s);
                        strcat(d,"$");
                        x = strlen(s);
                        printf("%s length => %i \n",s,x);
                }
                else
                {
                        printf("Cannot insert that word\n");
                }
                printf("Enter word\n");
                scanf("%s",s);
                x = strcmp(s,"quit");
        }
        printf("Final word is %s\n",d);
}
```

sttrcmp("abc","abc") would return 0 because they differ in 0 locations
strcmp("abc","xyz") would return non-zero

prog52.c   getchar and gets

/* as an exercise, remove the next line and compile and run */

```c
#include <stdio.h>
main ( )
{
        /* getchar returns one character from stdin as an integer*/
        /* gets returns one newline terminated line from stdin */
        /* the line is turned into a null terminated string with ws preserved */
        /* if the gets fails, it returns NULL, otherwise it returns the address that you passed
it */
        int i = 0;
        int c;
        char * ptr;
        char input_line[81];
        printf("Please enter string then press return \n");
        do
        {
                c = getchar( ):  /* a function that returns one character */
                input_line[i] = (char)c;
                i++;
        }
        while ( c != '\n' );

        input_line[i - 1] = '\0';          /* null terminate the line */
        printf("You entered %s\n" ,input_line);
        printf("\nPlease enter string then press return \n");
```

pointer to string returned   pointer to desired location to put string

```c
        ptr = gets(&input_line[0]);
        /* ptr = gets(inputline): THIS ALSO WORKS, WHY?? */
        if ( ptr == NULL )
                printf("gets failed \n");
        else
                printf("gets succeeded \n");

        printf("You entered %s\n",input_line);
}
```

prog53.c

```
#define        FALSE        0

#define        TRUE         1


#include <ctype.h>
```

HAVE A LOOK AT

ctype.h

LOOK at the macro

definitions

You'll find these in any C reference under ISxxxxx ususlly grouped together, or look up

ctype.h

```
main ( )

{

/* program to input characters and report whether they are alphabetic or not */

        char c =

        'x';

        char cr;

        while ( c !=

        'q' )

        {

                printf("\nEnter a character, I'll tell you if it's

                alphabetic\n");

                scanf("%c",&c);                /* get the character */

                scanf("%c",&cr);               /* soak in the carriage

return */

                if (isalpha(c) )

                        printf("%c is alp

                        habetic\n",c);

                else

                        printf("%c is not

                        alphabetic\n",c);

                printf("\n");

        }
```

}

String Functions

#include

<string.h>

char * strcat(sl,s2)   s2 stuck on end of s1, returns pointer to s1

char * strchr(s,c)   search s for 1st occurence of c, return pointer to c or NULL

int strcmp(sl,s2) 1   < 0   s1 < s2

                     0   s1 == s2

                    >0   s1 > s2

char * strcpy(sl,s2)   s2 copied over s1, returns pointer to s1

size_t strlen(sl)   find length of s1

char * strncat(s 1 ,s2,n)   copy s2 to end of s1 until null encountered or n chars copied

int strncmp(sl,s2,n)   compare s1 to s2 over n characters

char * strncpy(sl,s2,n)   copy s2 to s1 for at most n characters, may null terminate

before n

char * strrchr(s,c)   search s for last occurrence of c, returns pointer to c or NULL

1.   strcmp looks something like:

signed strcmp(const char *a.const char *b)

```
{
        while(*a=*b)
        {
                if(*a=='\O')
                return 0;
            a+
            +;
            b+
            +;
            }
        return
        *a-*b;
```

}

Character Functions

Most compilers actually implement these as macros not functions.

#include <ctype.h>

0	equates to no, false
1	equates to yes, true

isalnum(c)   is character c alphanumeric?

isalpha(c)   is character c alphabetic?

iscntrl(c)   is character c a control character?

isdigit(c)   is character c a digit?

islower(c)   is character c lower case?

isprint(c)   is character c a printable character

ispunct(c)   is character c a punctuation character

isupper(c)   is character c upper case?

isspace(c)   is character c a white space character?

tolower(c)   convert character c to lower case

toupper(c)   convert character c to upper case

Large Numbers as Characters Exercise

Write a C program to:

    read in, as character strings, two arbitrarily large numbers (ie: 37 digits)

    add them together

    display the result

```c
#include <stdio.h>
int
jconv(char);
char jrev(int);
 main()
{
              char num1[20], num2[20], num3 [21];
              int n1 [20], n2 [20] ;
              int n3 [21] ;
              int len1, len2,
              lenmax;
              int shuffle_dist, i;
              int ans, carry;

              for ( i = 0; i < 20; i++ )
              {
                 num1 [ i] = 0x00;
                 num2 [ i] = 0x00;
                 num3 [ i] = 0x00;
              }

              printf("Enter first number\n");
              scanf("%s",&num1[0]) ;
              printf("Enter second number\n");
              scanf("%s",&num2[0]) ;

              printf ("num1 char is %s \n", num1 ) ;
              printf ("num2 char is %s \n ", num2 ) ;

              /* find out how long the string is */
              len1 = strlen(num1);
              len2 = strlen(num2);
```

```c
/* find out which one is longer */
if ( len1 == len2 )
{
        /* you are okay, no shuffling required */
        /* just reverse the strings */
        printf("Strings are same length\n");
        lenmax = len1;

}
else
{
        if ( len1 < len2 )
        {
                printf("len1 < len2 \n" );
                lenmax = len2;
                printf("lenmax is %i \n",lenmax);
                shuffle_dist = len2 - len1;
                printf ("shuffle_dist is %i \n",
                shuffle_dist);
                /* need to shuffle lenl and pad with O's */
                for ( i = len1; i >= 0 ; i-- )
                        num1[i + shuffle_dist] = num1[i]
                 for ( l = 0; i < shuffle_dist; i++ )
                        num1 [i] =  'O';
        }
        else
        {
                printf("len1 > len2 \n");
                lenmax = len1;
                printf("lenmax is %i \n",lenmax);

                /* need to shuffle len2 and pad with O's */
                shuffle_dist = len1 - len2;
```

```
                              /* need to shuffle len1 and pad with O's */
                              for ( i = len2; i >= 0 ; i-- )
                                      num2[i + shuffle dist] = num2[i];
                              for ( i = 0; i < shuffle_dist; i++ )
                                      num2[i] = '0'; -

              }

      }


/*print after padding */
printf("after padding num1 is %s \n",num1);
printf("after padding num2 is %s \n",num2);


/* now convert from character to integer */
for ( i = 0; i < lenmax; i++ )
{
    n1[i] = jconv( num1[i] );
    n2[i] = jconv( num2[i] );
}
printf("after converting to array of integers \n")
for ( i = 0; i < lenmax; i++ )
{
              printf("%1i",n1[i]) ;
}
printf("\n") ;
for ( i = 0; i < lenmax; i++ )
{
              printf ("%1i" ,n2[i]);
}
/* now start adding from the back to the front */
carry =  0;
for ( i = lenmax - 1; i >= 0; i-- )
 {
    ans = n2[i] + n1[i] + carry;
    printf("ans is %i \n",ans);
    carry = ans / 10;
```

```
        n3 [i + 1] = ans % 10;
}
n3 [0]  = carry;
```

```c
printf("\n n3 array is \n");
for ( i = 0; i <= lenmax; i++ )
 {
                printf ("%1i" ,n3 [i]);
 }


/* now convert back to character */
for ( i = 0; i <= lenmax; i++ )
                num3[i] = jrev( n3[i] );
num3 [lenmax + 1] = '\0';
printf("Final string is %s \n",num3);

}
```

```c
int jconv(char c )
{
        switch ( c )
        {
            case '0':
                    return 0;
                    break;
            case '1':
                    return 1;
                    break;
            case '2':
                    return 2;
                    break;
            case '3':
                    return 3;
                    break;
            case '4':
                    return 4;
                    break;
            case '5':
                    return 5;
                    break;
            case '6':
                    return 6;
                    break;
            case '7':
                    return 7;
                    break;
            case '8':
                    return 8;
                    break;
            case '9':
                    return 9;
```

```c
                    break;
            }
}
char jrev(int i )
{
        switch ( i )
        {
          case 0:
                    return '0';
                    break;
          case 1:
                    return '1';
                    break;
          case 2:
                    return '2';
                    break;
          case 3:
                    return '3';
                    break;
          case 4:
                    return '4';
                    break;
          case 5:
                    return '5';
                    break;
          case 6:
                    return '6';
                    break;
          case 7:
                    return '7';
                    break;
          case 8:
                    return '8';
                    break;
          case 9:
                    return '9';
                    break;
        }
}
```

Solution to Characters as Large Integers Exercise

/* **charlarge.c** */

/* program to add together large character strings representing positive integers */

```c
#include <string.h>
#define        MAXDIGITS  20
char digits[ ] = { "0123456789"};
main ( )
{
        char sl[MAXDIGITS]; int lenl;  /* first string and its length */
        char s2[MAXDIGITS]; int len2; /* second string and its length */
        char sresult[MAXDIGITS];   /* result string */
        char dt1[2]; char dt2[2];        /* temporary strings for each digit */
        int dl, d2,dsum;                 /* temporary digits for integers */
        int i,maxlen,jpos;
        int carry_flag = 0;

        dtl[1] = 0x00;   /* null terminate the temporary strings */
        dt2[ 1] = 0x00;

        /* input the two strings to add together */
        printf("Enter first string \n");
        scanf("%s",s1);
        len1 = strlen(s1);
#ifdefDEBUG
        printf("There are %i digits in %s\n",lenl,sl);
#endif
        printf("Enter second string \n");
        scanf("%s" ,s2);
        len2 = strlen(s2);

#ifdef DEBUG
        printf("There are %i digits in %s\n",len2,s2);
#endif
```

```c
/* if the first string is longer, shuffle the second string into a field the
same size as the first string */
        if (lenl > len2 )
        {
#ifdef DEBUG
            printf("Shuffling s2\n");
#endif
            /* set maxlen and shuffle other number over */
            maxlen = len1;              /* pointer the last position in new s2, the null
*/
            jpos = len2;                /* pointer to last position in s2, the null * /

            /* start i at the null, move it back to zeroeth position
            */
            for (i = maxlen; i >= 0; i-- )
            {
                if (jpos >= 0 ) /* if orig char move to new */
                {
                    s2[i] = s2[jpos];
                    jpos--;
                }
                else    /* otherwise put in a zero */
                    s2[i] = '0';
            }
        }


/* if the second string is longer, shuffle the first string into a field the
                same size as the second string */
        else if ( len2 > len 1 )
        {
#ifdef DEBUG
            printf("Shuffling s 1\n ");
```

```
#endif
                /* set maxlen and shuffle other number over */
                maxlen = len2;   jpos = len1;
                for ( i  = maxlen; i >= 0; i-- )
                {
                        if ( jpos >= 0 )
                        {
                                sl[i] = s l[jpos];
                                jpos--;
                        }
                        else
                                s1[i] ='0';
                }
        }
        else
{
#ifdef
DEBUG
                printf("No need to shuffle \n");
#endif
                maxlen = len 1; }
#ifdef DEBUG
printf("s 1 now %s\n" ,s 1);
printf("s2 now %s\n" ,s2);
#endif


sresult[maxlen + 1] = OxOO;  /* put in the terminating null for sresult */
sresult[0] = ' ';                    /* assume a space in first position */

        for ( i = maxlen - 1; i >= 0 ; i-- )
        {
                dt1[0] = sl[i]; d1 =atoi(dtl); /* convert char to string, string to int */
                dt2[0] = s2[i]; d2 = atoi(dt2); /* convert char to string, string to int */
```

```c
        dsum = d1 + d2 + carry_flag;   /* compute resulting int */


        /* determine if a carry event occurred
        */
        if ( dsum >= 10 )
        {
                dsum = dsum - 10;
                carry flag = 1;
        else { carry flag = 0; }
#ifdef DEBUG
        printf("d 1 is %i ", d1);
        printf("d2 is %i\n",d2);
#endif
        sresult[i + 1] = digits[dsum];/* convert int to char via array */
    }
    if ( carry flag == 1 )
        sresult[0] = '1';   /* if the last addition produced a carry
                                put the 1 in the first position */
    printf("sresult is %s\n",sresult);
} /* end main */
```

Exercise 18

```
/* modify prog55.c so that it will allow the user to add new stocks to the stock list */
/* modify prog55.c so that the user can search for stocks by number */
/* allow them to enter the number and retrieve the name and ticker symbol */
```

prog55.c   Structures and Strings

```
#define       STRING_SIZE     20
#define       TICKER_SIZE     5
#define       MAX_ENTRIES     20


#include <string.h>
struct stock_entry
{
        int stock_number;
        char stock_name[STRING_SIZE];
        char ticker_symbol[TICKER_SIZE];
};


struct stock_entry
stock_list[MAX_ENTRIES] =
{
        { 0, "IBM", "IBM" },
        { 1, "General Motors", "GM" },
        { 2, "General Electric","GE"},
        { 3, "Terrill Owens", "MER" },
        { 4, "Ford","F" }
};
```

/* function to look for a string that matches the input string Search the array of structures

```c
                                                               for the
string.                Return index in array if found         Return -1 if not found. */
int find_stock( s, w, count)
struct stock_entry* s;
char * w;
int count;
{
        int     i, result;
        for ( i = 0; i < count;
        i++ )
        {
                result =
                strcmp(s(i).stock_name,w);
                if ( result == 0 )
                        return(i);             /* found it */
                result = strcmp(s[i].ticker_symbol,w);
                if ( result == 0 )
                        return(i);             /* found it */
        }
        return( -1);
}


 main ( )
{
        char
        search_word[STRING_SIZE];
        int idx;
        int  find_stock( );
        printf("\n\nEnter stock name or ticker symbol to search for (quit) to quit\n");


#ifdef SCANF
        scanf("%STRING _SIZEs", search_word);
#else
```

```c
        gets (search_ word);
#endif
        printf("You entered %s
        \1",search_word);
        /* strcmp returns 0 on a match */
        while ( strcmp(search_ word,"quit")
        {
                idx = find_stock(stock_list, search_word, 5);
                if ( idx == -1 )
                        printf("%s not found in stock_list \n",search_ word);
                else
                        printf("%i %s % s\n ", stock_list[idx].stock_number,
                                stock_list[idx].stock_name, stock_list[idx].ticker symbol):
                printf("\n\nEnter stock name or ticker symbol to search for (quit) to quit\n");
#ifdef SCANF
                scanf(" %STRING _SIZEs " ,search_word);
#else
                gets (search_ word);
#endif
                printf("You entered %s \t" ,search_word);
        }
        printf("\n\n");
} /* end main */
```

Enter stock name or ticker symbol to search for (quit) to quit

ibm

You entered ibm   ibm not found in stock_list

Enter stock name or ticker symbol to search for (quit) to quit

IBM

You entered IBM   0   IBM   IBM

Enter stock name or ticker symbol to search for (quit) to quit

Terrill

You entered Terrill   Terrill not found in stock_list

Enter stock name or ticker symbol to search for (quit) to quit
Terrill Owens
You entered Terrill Owens   Terrill Owens not found in stock_list

Enter stock name or ticker symbol to search for (quit) to quit
quit
You entered quit

acc prog55.c   /* to not have debug prints */
ace -DSCANF prog55.c /* to have debug prints */

prog57.c Pointers

```c
/* Program to illustrate pointers */
main ( )
{
        int i;
        int j;
        int * int pointer; /* read as intpointer is a pointer to an integer * /
        /* int_pointer gets address of i  * /
        /* intpointer now points at memory location that variable */
        /* i is stored in */
        int_pointer = &i;

        /* assign 5 to the location that int pointer is pointing to */
        /* this effectively assigns 5 to i */
        /* and is equivalent to i = 5; */
        *int_pointer = 5;

        /* assign to j the value pointed to by int pointer */
        /* this is equivalent to j = i; */
        j = *int_pointer;
        printf("i = %i, j = %i\n",i,j);
}
```

prog58.c   Pointers

```c
/* Program to illustrate pointers */
main( )
{
        /* declare a character variable c, assign initial value! */
        charc = 'Q';
        char d = 'x';
        /* declare a character pointer char_pointer */
        /* assign it the address of the character variable c */
        /* char_pointer now points to c */
        char * char_pointer = &c;
        char * dptr = &d;
        char ** ddptr = &dptr;
        char *** dddptr = &ddptr;

        /*printf("%c %c\n",c, *char_pointer);*/
        printf("%c %c %c %c \n",d,*dptr,**ddptr,***dddptr);
        printf("address of d    %p value of d %c \n",&d,d);
        printf("address of dptr %p value of dptr %x \n",&dptr,dptr);
        printf("address of ddptr %p value of ddptr %x \n",&ddptr,ddptr);
        printf("address of dddptr %p value of dddptr %x \n",&dddptr,dddptr);

        /* assign a new value to c using traditional method */
        c = '/';
        printf("%c %c\n",c, *char_pointer);

        /* assign a new value to c using pointer method */
        *char _pointer = '(';
        printf("%c %c\n",c, *char_pointer);

/* sample output */
xxxx
address of d      f7fffcge value of d      x
address of dptr f7fffc94 value of dptr f7fffcge
address of ddptr f7fffc90 value of ddptr f7fffc94
address of dddptr f7fffc8c value of dddptr f7fffc90
//
( (
```

Pointers

char c = 'Q'; | Q | addr 102

char d = 'x'; | x | addr 103

char * dptr = &d;· | 103 | addr 104

char * * ddptr = & dptr; | 104 | addr 108

char * * * dddptr = & ddptr; | 108 | addr 112

d=>x   &d => 103

dptr => 103   *dptr => x   &dptr => 104

ddptr => 104   *ddptr => 103

                        **ddptr => x

                        &ddptr => 108

dddptr=> 108   *dddptr => 104

                        **ddptr => 103

                        ***dddptr => x

                        &dddptr => 112

prog59.c   Pointers to Structures

```
/* program for debt trade manipulation */
/* let's assume that they cannot be traded on certain days, i.e. Christmas */
/* let's refer to the structures via pointers */
main ( ) {
        int i;
        struct debt_trade        {
                int day;
                int month;
                int year;
                float price;
                float par;        };
        struct debt_trade        debts[5];
        struct debt_trade *      dtptr;
        dtptr = &debts[0];        /* establish pointer to first element of array */
        for (i = 0; i < 5; i++ )
        {
                scanf("%i %i %i %f %f",&debts[i].day, &debts[i].month,
                        &debts[i].year, &debts[i].price,&debts[i].par);


                /* see if date is any good using array notation */
                if (debts[i].day = 25 && debts[i].month = 12 )
                        printf("%f %f CANNOT TRADE ON %i/%i/%i\n", debts[i].price,
                                debts[i] .par, debts[i] .day,debts[i].month,debts[i) .year);
                else
                        printf("%f %f okay on %i/%i/%i", debts[i].price, debts[i].par,
                debts[i] .day, debts[i].month, debts[i]. year);


                /* see if date is any good using pointer notation */
                if ( dtptr->day = 25 && dtptr->month = 12 )
                        printf("%f %f CANNOT TRADE ON %i/%i/%i\n", debtsj il.price,
                debts[i] .par, debts[i] .day,debts[i].month,debts[i). year);
```

```c
/* see if date is any good using pointer and array notation */
if (dtptr->day == 25 && debts[i].month == 12 )
        printf("%f %f CANNOT TRADE ON %i/%i/%i\n", debts[ i].price,
        debts[i].par,  debts[i].day,debts[i].month, debts[i].year):


/* move the pointer ahead to next entry
*/
dtptr++;
} /* end for */
```

prog59.dat

1 1 1992 1.0 1.0

1 1 1993 123.5 1.07

2 28 1993 34.5 1.098

25 12 1980 1.0 1.98

23 111979 100.532.73

Sample Run

a.out < prog59.dat

1.000000 1.000000 okay on 1/1/1992

123.500000 1.070000 okay on 1/1/1993

34.500000 1.098000 okay on 2/28/1993

1.000000 1.980000 CANNOT TRADE ON 25/12/1980

1.000000 1.980000 CANNOT TRADE ON 25/12/1980

1.000000 1.980000 CANNOT TRADE ON 25/12/1980

100.5299992.730000 okay on 23/11/1979

A better linked list example

```c
struct node
{
 int  val;

 int valsq;
 struct node * next;
};

#include <stdio.h>
void main( )
{
        struct node * head=NULL;
        int v;

        printf("enter a positive val or -1 to end \n");
        scanf("%i",&v);
        while(v! = -1 )
          {
                    addnode(v, &head);
                    printlist(head);
                    printf("next... ");
                    scanf("%i",&v);
          }
        /* list after loop */
        printlist(head);
}

void addnode(int in, struct node **h)
{
  struct node *p;
  p=*h;

  /* go through list till find value or reach end */
  while(p!=NULL && p->val! = in)
      p=p->next;

  /* if end was reached add_item at head of list */
  if(p == NULL)
    {
        /* allocate new node and copy data */
        p = (struct node*) malloc(sizeof(struct node));
        p->val=in;
        p->valsq = in * in;

        /* make this node point at top item in list */
    p->next=*h;
```

```c
/* reset head to be this new node */
*h=p;
    }
}

void printlist(struct node *h)
{
  /* repeat while pointer is not null */
  while(h)
  {
  /* print value at this node */
  printf(" %i\t%i\n" ,h ->val,h ->valsq);

  /* print next node * I
        h=h->next;
    }
}
```

prog60.c Using Pointers in a Linked List

```
/* also demonstrates dynamic memory allocation with malloc */
/* we need to read in numbers, don't know how many */
#include <stdlib.h>
#include <stdio.h>
main ( )
{
        /* a linked list entry structure definition */
        struct lle
        {
                int     value;          /* value in list */
                int     squared value; /* value in list */
                struct lle *next;       /* pointer to next entry */
        };
        struct lle      first_element; /* first entry in list */
        struct lle* next_element;       /* pointer to any entry in list */
        int val;

        printf("size of lle is %i\n",sizeof(first_element));
        printf("Enter value to square and store (-1) to stop\n");
        scanf("%i",&val);

        /* set up pointer to already established element */
        next_element = &first_element;
        /* enter value to square
        and store */
        while (val!= -1 )
        {
                next_element->value = val;
                next_element->squared_ value = val * val;

                /* allocate memory for another structure */
```

```c
        /* returns a pointer to the memory allocated, pointer will be of type
        (char *) */
        next_element->next = (struct lle*) malloc(sizeof(first_element)):
        printf("Enter value to square and store (-1) to
        stop\n");
        scanf("%i",&val);
        if(val !=-1)
                next_element = next_element->next;
        else
                next_element->next = NULL;
}
next_element =
&first_element;

while (next element != NULL)
{
        /* print out values from this linked list element * /
        printf("value = %i squared %i\n",
                next_element->value, next_element->squared , value);
                printf("\t This record stored at        %p\n",next_element);
        printf("\t This record points to record at %p\n\n",next_element->next);

        /* advance pointer to next element in linked list */
        next_element = next_element->next;
}
}
```

valref.c Pointers and Functions

/* demonstrate that if a function receives the address of an item it can

update the item. This is roughly equivalent to call by reference, but it still

is call by value, the value passed is the address of another item */


```
#ifdef ANSI
        void refl(int* x)        /* ansi function header */
#else
        void refl(x)             /* K & R function header */
int*  x;
#endif
{
        *x = *x + 1;                     /* add one to value stored at address stored in x */
        printf("In refl  x = %i \n",*x);  /* print it out */
        return;
}


main ( )
{
        int i  = 5;
        printf("In main i = %i \n",i);
        refl(&i);                        /* pass address of i to refl */
        printf("In main i = %i \n",i);   /* notice that refl changed i */
}
```

Exercise 19

/* FOR THOSE COMFORTABLE WITH THE LINKED LIST DATA STRUCTURE */

/* write a C program to allow

1:      User to input elements into a linked list

2:      User to print linked list forwards

3:      User to add elements to end of linked list

4:      User to delete any element from list (if it is present) by searching for the

first

occurrance of the value and deleting that item.

implement as you deem fit (double linked list)

*/

/* FOR THOSE WHO WOULD PREFER TO DO SOMETHING

DIFFERENT */

/*

Write A C Program that will do the following

1)   Input text up to 1,024 characters into an

array

2)   Create a structure that stores

# of characters

# of white space seperated words

longest word

shortest word

3)   Allow user to search for any string in the array

if found, allow them to change it

to some other string without

damaging

the characters around the point

of

editing and without producing

any

new whitespace

USEFUL FUNCTIONS

iswspace(c)

strstr(s 1 ,s2)

/* ex19.c */

```c
/* solution to exercise 19 */
#include <stdio.h>
#include <stdlib.h>
#include  <string.h>
#include <malloc.h>
 struct lle
{
      char value [10] ;
      struct lle * p;
};


/* functions will be given pointer to head of list */
/* functions will return pointer to head of list */
struct lle * add_item(struct lle *);
struct lle * delete_item(struct lle *);

      /* function accepts pointer to head of list and returns nothing */
      void print_list (struct lle *);

      main()
      {
      int choice;
      struct lle * hptr = NULL;
      for ( ; ; )
      {
            printf("\nDo you want to \n");
            printf("l add an item\n");
```

214

```c
        printf("2 delete an item\n");
        printf("3 print list\n");
        printf ("4 quit\n");
        scanf("%i",&choice) ;

        switch(choice)
        {
                case 1:
                        hptr = add_item (hptr) ;
                        break;
                case 2:
                        hptr = delete_item(hptr);
                        break;

                case 3:
                        print_list (hptr) ;
                        break;

                case 4:
                        printf ("Good-bye\n") ;
                        exit(l) ;

                default:
                        printf ("Good-bye\n") ;
                        exi t (-1) ;
                }
    } /* end forever loop */
} /* end main */
struct lle * add_item(struct lle * ptr)
{
    char word[50]
    ;
    struct lle *
```

```
tmp;
struct lle * original_head = ptr;
printf("Enter string to enter\n");
scanf ("%s", &word [0] ) ;
while ( strlen(word) > 20 )
{
            printf("Word too long, 20 chars max\n");
            scanf("%s",&word[0]) ;
}
/* is the list currently empty? */
if ( ptr == NULL )
{
            /* we are at the head of the list */
            /* get more memory */
            tmp = (struct lle * ) malloc sizeof(struct lle) );
            /* make sure the malloc worked */
            if ( tmp === NULL )
            {
                        printf("malloc failed\n");
                        exi t (- 2) ;
            }
            /* assign value and pointer */
            strcpy(tmp->value,word) ;
            tmp->p = NULL;

            /* return new head of list */
            return ( tmp );
}
```

```c
        /* traverse the list */
        while ( ptr->p != NULL)
        {
            ptr = ptr->p;
        }
        /* at this point in time, ptr is at the end of the list */


        /* get more memory */
        tmp = (struct lle * ) malloc ( sizeof(struct lle) );
        /* make sure the malloc worked */
        if ( tmp == NULL )
        {
                    printf("malloc failed\n");
                    exi t (- 2) ;
        }
        /* add newly created tail item to list */
        ptr->p = tmp;
        strcpy(tmp->value,word) ;
        tmp->p = NULL;
        return (original_head) ;
}

struct lle * delete_item(struct lle * ptr)
{
        char word[50];
        struct lle * pl;
        struct lle * tmp;

        /* is there anything In the list? */
        if ( ptr == NULL )
        {
            printf("There are no items in list\n");
            /* return that list is still empty */
```

```c
    return (NULL) ;
}
printf("Enter string to delete\n");
scanf ("%s", &word [0]) ;
while ( strlen(word) > 20 )
{
    printf ("Word too long, 20 chars max\n") ;
    scanf("%s",&word[0]) ;
}


/* is it at the head of the list? */
if strcmp(ptr->value,word) == 0)
{
    /* it is at the head of the list */
    /* is this a singleton? */
    if ( ptr->p == NULL)
    {
                /* give the memory back */
                free (ptr) ;
                /* list is now empty */
                return (NULL) ;
    }
    else
    {
        /* return the pointer field of the head  as the new head */
        tmp = ptr->p;
        free (ptr) ;
        return (tmp) ;

        /* traverse list to find item */
        tmp = ptr;        /* save the head of the list */
        pl = ptr;         /* save the current position */
        ptr = ptr->p;     /* get the next position */
```

```c
            while ( ptr  != NULL )
            {
                    if ( strcmp(ptr->value,word) == 0 )
                    {
                            /* delete the item */
                            pl->p = ptr->p;
                            free (ptr) ; /* give the memory back */
                            return (tmp) ; /* return original pointer */
                    }
                    ptr = ptr->p;
                    pl = pl->p;
            }

        /* if we got here then the word was not in the list */
        printf("Item not in list \n");
        return(tmp);  /* return original head *
        }

void print_list (struct lle * ptr)
{
        if ( ptr == NULL )
        {
                printf("list is empty\n");
                return;
        }
        /* traverse the list printing things as you go */
        while ( ptr != NULL)
        {
                printf ("%s  ", ptr->value);
                ptr = ptr->p;
        }
        return;

}
```

prog76.c getchar & putchar

/* program to read and echo characters until * /

/* end of file (EOF) is encountered */

/* two ways to run this program */

/* 1: run it from the terminal prog76 */

/* type in your input, press control d for EOF */

/* 2: run it from the terminal prog76 < input file */

/* provide the name of an input file and redirect * /

/* the input to come from that file using UNIX stdin */

/* when EOF is encountered, program will terminate */

/* you don't need to put any special EOF character

        in the data file, system will figure it out */


```c
#include <stdio.h>
main ( )
{
        /* even though we are reading in characters */
        /* we need c to be declared as an int because getchar returns an int * /
        int c;
        c = getchar( );
        while (c != EOF)
        {
                /* echo the input character to stdout */
                putchar(c);

                /* get the next char from stdin */
                c = getchar( );
        }
}
```

prog77.c   fopen, fprintf, fclose, getc, putc

/* program to copy one file to another * /

/* and that cleans up after itself, not counting on the os */


```c
#define  FILENAME_SIZE   40
#include <stdio.h>
main ( )
{
        char source[FILENAME_SIZE], dest[FILENAME_SIZE];
        FILE *in, *out;
        int c;
        int char_count = 0;

        printf("Enter source file name:");
        scanf("%39s", source);
        printf(t'You entered %s as file to copy from\n",source);
        in = fopen(source,"r");
        if ( in == NULL )
        {
                printf("Cannot open %s \n",source);
                exit(-1);
        }

        printf("Enter dest filename: ");
        scanf("%39s", dest);
        printf("You entered %s as file to create\n",dest);
        out = fopen(dest,"w");
        if (out == NULL)
        {
                printf("Cannot open %s \n",dest);
                fclose(in);
                exit(-2);
```

```
        }

        /* write the name of the source file as first line in output file */
        fprintf(out,"SOURCE FILE NAME WAS %s\n",source);

        /* write the name of the source file as first line in output file */
        fprintf(out,"Dest FILE NAME WAS %s\n",dest);

        c = getc(in);
        while (c != EOF)
        {
                char_count++;
                putc(c,out);
                c = getc(in);
        }
        fprintf(out,"SOURCE FILE HAD %i CHARACTERS\n",char_count);
        printf("File copy complete \n");

        /* close the files explicitly */
        fclose(in);
        fclose( out);
}
```

Enter name of file to be copied: prog74.dat
You entered prog74.dat as file to copy from
Enter name of output file: out.1
You entered out.l as file to create
File copy complete

cat out.l
SOURCE FILE NAME WAS prog74.dat
Dest FILE NAME WAS out.1
the alphabet abcdefghijklmnopqrstuvwxyz
the alphabet abcdefghijklmnopqrstuvwxyz
the alphabet abcdefghijklmnopqrstuvwxyz
the alphabet abcdefghijklmnopqrstuvwxyz
the alphabet abcdefghijklmnopqrstuvwxyz
the alphabet abcdefghijklmnopqrstuvwxyz
the alphabet abcdefghijklmnopqrstuvwxyz
the alphabet abcdefghijklmnopqrstuvwxyz
SOURCE FILE HAD 320 CHARACTERS

uitp.c

This program shows file i/o and string processing

The input and output files are shown below

If you can follow this code, you have mastered the material to this point

```
Open a flat data file, create two seperate files
        one flat file for further fixed sized processing
        one space delimited file for numeric
        processing
#include <stdio.h>
#include <stdlib.h>
 main( )
{
        int ia, il , i2;
        double xbid, xoffer;
        char type[3]; /* three character field for type of transaction */
        char temp[20];   /* 20 character field for temporary string operations */
        /* read directly into here using fixed sizes from file */
        struct {
                char transact[l];
                char cusip[8];
                char date[8];
                char bid[10];
                char offer[ 10];
                char mlnumber[5];
                char mlsymbol[6];
                char name[30];
                char misc[8];
                char cr;
        } rec;

        FILE *fp l, *fp2, *fp3;        /* file pointers for reading from and writing to */
```

```
int x;
/* START OF EXECUTABLE CODE */
il = 0; i2 = 0;


/* open the price.file for reading */
if ( (fpl = fopen("price.file","r") ) == NULL)
{
        printf ("CAN NOT open input file (price.file ) \n");
        exit(100);

}


/* open the pricedadd.input file for writing, if it exists overwrite it */
if ( (fp2 = fopen("priceadd.input","w") ) == NULL) {
        printf ("CAN NOT open output file (priceadd.input)
        \n");
        exit(200); }


/* open the priceupd.input file for writing, if it exists overwrite it
*/
if ( (fp3 = fopen("priceupd.input","w") ) == NULL){
        printf ("CAN NOT open output file (priceupd.input) \n");
        exit(300); }


/* read in 86 data characters and one carriage return from file */
/* pointer to destination, size of each thing to be read ( in bytes)
count of things to be read, file pointer of file to be read from */
x = fread(char *)&rec,1,87,fpl);
/* while not end of file */
while( !feof(fpl) )
  {
        rec.cr = '\0';    /* convert the carriage return to a null */
        printf("%s \n",&rec); /* print out the whole record */
        printf("%c \n" ,rec. transact[0]): /* stdout is standard output stream */
```

```
fwrite(&rec.cusip[0], 1,8,stdout); /* print out each field, one per line */
putc('\n' ,stdout);        /* add a lf to the output stream */


fwrite(&rec.date[0], 1,8,stdout);
putc('\n' ,stdout);
fwrite(&rec.bid[0],l, 10,stdout);
putc('\n' ,stdout);
fwrite(&rec.offer[0], 1, 10,stdout);
putc('\n' ,stdout);
fwrite(&rec.mlnumber[0],1,5,stdout);
putc('\n' ,stdout);
fwrite(&rec.mlsymbol[0],1,6,stdout);
putc('\n' ,stdout);
fwrite(&rec.name[0],1,30,stdout);
putc('\n' .stdout);
putc('\n' ,stdout);


if ( rec.transact[0] == 'A')
{
        i1 = i1 + 1;     /* add one to i1 */
        type[0] = rec.mlsymbol[0];  /*transfer mlsymbol to type */
        type[1] = rec.mlsymbol[l];
        type[2] = rec.mlsymbol[2];
        /* builld up the output file for adds, no delimiters */
        fwrite( &rec.cusip[0], 1 ,8,fp2);
        fwrite(&rec.date[0],1,8,fp2);
        fwrite(&rec.date[0],1,8,fp2);
        fwrite(&rec.mlnumber[0], 1,5,fp2);
        fwrite(&rec.mlsymbol[0],1,6,fp2);
        fwrite(&type[0],1,3,fp2);
        fwrite(&rec.name[0],1,30,fp2);


        /* stick a carriage return on the end of output record*/
```

```
        putc('\n' ,fp2);
    }
```

```c
        if ( rec.transact[0] == 'U')
         {
                i2 = i2 + 1; /*  add one to i2 */
                strncpy(&temp[0] ,&rec.bid[0], 10);  /* transfer bid to temp */
                temp[10] = '\0';                       /* tack on a null */
                xbid = atof(temp);                     /* convert to float */
                xbid = xbid / 100000;
                strncpy(&temp[0],&rec.offer[0],10); /* transfer offer to temp */
                temp[10] = '\0';           /* tack on a null */
                xoffer = atof(temp);    /* convert to float */
                xoffer = xoffer / 100000;

                /* build up output file for updates, space delimiters */
                fwrite(&rec.cusip[0], 1,8,fp3);
                putc(' ',fp3);
                fwrite(&rec.date[0],1,8,fp3);
                putc(' ',fp3);
                fprintf(fp3,"%10.5f %10.5f\n",xbid,xoffer);
         }

            /* get the next record */
            fread((char *)&rec,1,87,fp1);
/* end while */
printf("i1 = %d\n",i1);
printf("i2 = %d\n",i2);
    fclose(fp1);
    fclose(fp2);
    fclose(fp3);
}
```

price.file **used for input**

U459145 101993030800948680000097803000094CD9AACOlllBF, AUSTRALIAN DOLLAR BOND 00000000

A459145 101 99303080094868000009780300094CD9AACOlllB F, AUSTRALIAN DOLLAR BOND 00000000

U4591453019930308010S5550000109101000962F3ACC026IBF, MULTICURRENCY SERIES 026 00000000

ULGLAKlUG 1 9930308{)()()()()()(AKJHACC8011ST SUPPLEMENTAL INCREASE FOR 00000000

UDLHJHLJG 1 9930308000000000000000000GDLGACC8022ND SUPPLEMENTAL DEPOSIT FOR 00000000

U62623K2219930308010945000011509800094B73ALML3HMUN INV TR FD 3H AL 00000000

.U62623K3319930308008617700000911070000094B81ALML3JMUN INV TR FD 3J AL 00000000

U62623K6319930308008997000000946090000094DJ4ALML3NMUN INV TR FD 3N AL 00000000

U62623L391993030801 07348000011 268200094DN2ALML3VMUN INY TR FD 3V AL 00000000

U62623L5819930308010961000011564800094DP7ALML3YMUN INV TR FD 3Y AL 00000000

U62623M4019930308011110000011624100094DWIALMI.AGMUN INV TR FD 4G AL 00000000

U62623N7919930308010964700011466300094D59ALMIAWMUN INV TR FD 4W AL 00000000

U4591452019930308009543500000968890009DBLOAMLOOlIBF FST CTS AUST. FGN HLDR 1\E00000000

U4591452319930308009537300000968260009DBLIAMLOO2IBF FST CTS AUST-2FGN HLDR 1\E00000000

U4591452519930308009738400000988670009DBL2AMLOO3AUSSIE MOKI'GAGELINK SERIES 3 00000000

U62623R7119930308010532500011131600094J52AMT001MUN INV TR FD AMT 001 MPS 00000000

U62623T2619930308010528700011077500094J53AMTOO2MUN INV TR FD AMT 002 MPS 00000000

U62623TS4199303080099206000010497700094J54AMT003MUN INV TR FD AMT 003 MPS 00000000

U62623T65 199303080091926000009719400094J55AMTOO4MUN INV TR FD AMT 004 MPS 00000000

U62623UI 71993030801 09282000011 539800094J56AMTOOSMUN INV TR FD AMT 005 MPS 00000000

U62623U1919930308009596500010145200094J57AMTOO6M TR FD AMT 006 MPS 00000000

U62623U4919930308010725300011349500094J58AMTOO7MITR FD AMT 007 MPS 00000000

U62623V4519930308010710900011333400094J59AMT008MITR FD AMT 008 MPS 00000000

U62623V5319930308010587800011180000094J60AMTOO9MITR FD AMT 009 MPS 00000000

U62623V8019930308010850100011462600094J61AMTOIOMITR FD AMT 010 MPS 00000000

U62623V8419930308008850700009342300094J62AMT011MITR FD AMT 011 MPS 00000000

U62623V8519930308010682100011285700094J63AMTOI212TH AMT SERIES 00000000

U62623W851993030801 063980000 11253200094J64AMTO 1313TH AMT SERIES 00000000

U62623X2019930308010796500011424500094J65AMTOI4MITF 14TH AMT 00000000

U62623XI919930308010777400011404000094J66AMTOI5MITF 15TH AMT 00000000

priceadd.input created by uitp.c

45914510199303081993030894CD9AACOllAACIBF,AUSTRALIANDOLLARBOND

priceupd.input created by uitp.c

45914510 19930308 948.68000 978.03000

4591453019930308 1055.55000 1091.01000

LGLAKHJG 19930308 0.00000 0.00000

DLH.JHLJG 19930308 0.00000 0.00000

62623K22 19930308 1094.50000 1150.98000

62623K3319930308 861.77000 911.07000

62623K6319930308 899.70000 946.09000

62623L39 19930308 1073.48000 1126.82000

62623L58 19930308 1096.10000 1156.48000

62623M40 19930308 1111.00000 1162.41000

62623N79 19930308 1096.47000 1146.63000

4591452019930308 954.35000 968.89000

45914523 19930308 953.73000 968.26000

45914525 19930308 973.84000 988.67000

62623R71 19930308 1053.25000 1113.16000

62623T26 19930308 1052.87000 1107.75000

62623T54 19930308 992.06000 1049.77000

62623T65 19930308 919.26000 971.94000

62623U17 19930308 1092.82000 1153.98000

62623U19 19930308 959.65000 1014.52000

62623U49 19930308 1072.53000 1134.95000

62623V45 19930308 1071.09000 1133.34000

62623V53 19930308 1058.78000 1118.00000

62623V80 19930308 1085.01000 1146.26000

62623V84 19930308 885.07000 934.23000

62623V85 19930308 1068.21000 1128.57000

62623W85 19930308 1063.98000 1125.32000

62623X20 19930308 1079.65000 1142.45000

62623X19 19930308 1077.74000 1140.40000

argtest.c

```c
/* program to access command line arguments * /
#include <stdio.h>
/* void main(int argc, char * argv[])    ANSI version */
main ( argc, argv )      /* K & R version */
int argc;                /* count of the number of commands on the command line */
char * argv[];           /* the arguments as strings */
{
        int i  = 0;
        printf("Arg count argc => %i\n",argc);
        printf("Command line args are \n");
        /* while (argv[i] ) also works */
        while (argv[i] != NULL )
        {
                printf("argv[%i] => %s\n",i,argv[i]);
                i++;
        }
        exit(0);
}
```

run this program by typing:

a.out

a.out 1 2 3

a.out dog cat bird hello kitty

and see what output you get

it'll explain argc and argv completely

argc, argv, envp

argc   count of arguments on command line

argv   array of strings, parsed command line

envp   array of strings, parsed environment

ex12 filel file2

argc   3

argv

ex12 \0

                filel \0

                file2 \0

                null

envtest.c C Interface to UNIX Environment

/* program to access command line arguments, program to access environment variables */

```c
#include <stdio.h>
main ( argc, argv, envp )
int argc;
char * argv[];
char * envp [];
{
        int env _count = 0;
        while ( envp[env _count] !=
        NULL)
        {
                printf("%s\n" ,envp[env _count]);
                env _count++;
        }
        exit(0);
}
```

DISPLAY=:O
DSQUERY=SYBASE
FONTPATH=/usr/openwin/lib/fonts
FRAMEBUFFER=/dev/fb
HELPPATH=/usr/openwin/lib/help
HOME=/usr/jtk
LD _LIBRARY _PATH=/usr/openwin/lib
LOGNAME=jtk
MANPATH=/usr/openwin/share/man:/usr/man
NEWSSERVER=2457 672469 .2000;spd21
OPENWINHOME=/usr/openwin
PATH=/usr/jtk/bin:/usr/openwin/bin/xview:/usr/openwin/b
        in:
        /usr/local/bin:/usr/local/lang:/usr/local/sybase/bin:
        /usr/uc b:/usr /bin:/usr/etc:. :/usr/5bin
PWD=/usr/local/jtk/jtk/C/myCprograms
SHELL=/bin/csh
SYBASE=/usr/local/sybase
TERM=sun
USER=jtk
WINDOW _PARENT=/dev/winO
WMGR_ENV _PLACEHOLDER=/dev/win3
XAPPLRES D IR=/usr/openwin/lib/X 11/app-defaults
TERMCAP=sun-cmd:te=\E[>4h:ti=\E[>4l:tc=sun:

exercise 20

/* write a C program that will copy one file to another file */

/* the user should enter the file names from the command line */

/* optional brain teaser * /

/* allow the user to enter file names from the command line OR

if they don't put any file names on the command line

prompt them for the file names */

/* optional brain buster */

/* allow the user to copy one file to multiple files simultaneously */

/* is there a limit to how many output files they can create??? */

sol20.c

```c
#include <stdlib.h>
#include <stdio.h>
/* argc is count of number of command line arguments */
/* argv is array of strings each string is one of the command line arguments */
void do_copy(char * s, char * d)
{
        FILE * in, *out;
        int c;
        in = fopen(s,"r");
        if (in == NULL)
        {
                printf("Cannot open %s \n",s);
                exit(-1);
        }
        out = fopen(d,"w");
        if ( out == NULL)
        {
                printf("Cannot open %s \n",d);
                exit(-2);
        }
        while ( ( c = getc(in) != EOF )
                        putc(c,out);
        fclose(in);
        fclose(out);
}

int main(int argc, char * argv[] )
{
        int i;
        char dest[20],source[20];
        if ( argc == 1 )
        {
```

```c
        printf("Please enter source filenmae \n");
        scanf("%s", source);
        printf("Please enter dest filename \n");
        scanf("%s" .dest);
}
else if ( argc == 2 )
{

        strcpy(source,argv[l]);
        printf("Please enter dest filename \n");
        scanf("%s" ,dest);
}
if ( argc >= 3 )
{
        for ( i = 2; i < argc; i++ )
        {
                do_copy(argv[1],argv[i]);
        }
else
        do _ copy( source,dest);

printf("File copy complete \n");
}
```

prog78.c Storage Qualifiers register, const,volatile

```c
/* program to introduce storage qualifiers */
main ( )
{
        /* i will be local to this routine * /
        /* it will be on the stack if there is room * /
        /* otherwise it will be in data area of routine */
        int i;

        /* buffer will be local to this routine */
        /* it will be on the stack if there is room */
        /* otherwise it will be in data area of routine */
        /* this declaration automatically consumes 80 bytes of data */
        char buffer[80];

        /* b_ptr is local to this routine */
        /* it can point to a string of arbitrary length */
        /* it consumes only sizeof(char * ) */
        /* the area holding the string will be managed by the
        system, perhaps being dynamically allocated
        and deallocated as space requirements change */
        char * b_ptr;

        /* want these variables in registers if possible */
        /* perhaps i will be used as a loop counter */
        /* putting it in a register will produce faster execution */
        register int i;

        /* text_pointer will be used in repeated string
                operations, putting it in a register
                will speed execution * /
        register char * text pointer;
```

```
/* want these variables in read only memory */
/* want to make sure their value doesn't change */
/* during execution of program */
/* they will not be on the stack */
/* they are local to this routine */
const double pi = 3.141592654;
const char *cp = &buffer[0];


/* want to prevent compiler from removing */
/* optimizations of code * /
/* if I did not have the volatile keyword here, the
        compiler would remove the second statement
        shown at location A below * /
volatile char * out port;


/* assign initial address to text pointer */
/* it now points to the zeroeth byte of the character array buffer * /
text pointer = &buffer[0];


/* i  and text pointer are in registers */
/* faster execution */
  for ( i = 0; i < 80; i++ )
        *text_pointer++ = 0x00;
```

```
/* LOCATION A */
/* this is code that is typical in device drivers
        of communication software, you want to write
        to bytes in a row to some chip through its port address */
/* an optimizing compiler would think that you
        changed the value at outport to OxOa and
        then changed it to OxOd, thus the first
        statement changing it to OxOa has no value,
        therefore an optimizing compiler would remove the
        first statement from the executable */
/* the compiler would think that the first */
/* assignment is useless and would optimize */
/* it out of the code */
/* the volatile prevents this */
/* if out port was assigned to coml port Ox2f8 */
/* and I said */
/*  *out_port = OxOa; */
/*  *out_port = OxOd; */

}
```

speedl.c   Typical Inefficient Code

```
/* demonstrates some "usual" (and inefficient) ways things are done */
#ifdef          SPEED 1
main ( )
{
        int k.l:
        char buffer[2001];
        for ( k = 0; k < 10000; k++ )
        {
                for ( l = 0; l < 2000; l++ )
                {
                        buffer[l] = 0x00;
                }
        }
}
/* time to run 19.4u O.Os 0: 19 99% 0+132k O+Oio Opf+Ow */
#endif


/* compare the run time statistics for SPEED1 to SPEED2 (on next page ) */
```

```
#ifdef SPEED2
/* speed2.c */
/* demonstrates "faster" way things are done by more experienced programmers */
main ( )
{
        register int k;
        register int i;
        register char * b_ptr;
        char buffer[200 1];
        for (k = 0; k < 10000; k++)
        {
                b_ptr = &buffer[0];
                for (i = 0; i < 2000; i++ )
                {
                        *b_ptr++ = 0x00;
                }
        }
}
#endif
```

14.6u 0.0s 0:14 99% 0+132k O+Oio Opf+Ow

13.2u 0.0s 0: 13 99% 0+ 132k O+Oio Opf+Ow

10.0u 0.0s 0:10 99% 0+ 132k O+Oio Opf+Ow

7.6u 0.0s 0:08 99% 0+ 132k O+Oio Opf+Ow

prog64.c copying strings using pointers

```
/* prog64.c copying strings using pointers */
/* this routine uses a pointer to specify where the data comes from
        and a pointer to specify where the data is supposed to end up
        it also uses pointer arithmetic in the copying loop,
        it has an inefficiency: whose correction is shown
                the test *from != '\0' is unneccessary
*/
void copy_l (to, from)
char *to, *from;
{
        for ( ; *from != '\0'; from++, to++ )
                        *to = *from;
        *to = '\0';
}


/* copying strings using pointers is most efficient method
        effectively uses pointer arithmetic and implied tests */
void copy_2 ( to, from )
char *to, *from;
{
        /* remember C is an expression language and each statement
                        returns a value. In this case, we can use that
                        value to make our code more concise */
#if 0
        while ( *from )
                *to++ = *from++;
        *to = '\0';
#endif
        while ( *to++ = *from++ ) ;


char s 1 [] = "Terrill Owens";
```

```
char s2[40]; char s3[40];
char s4[40]; char s5[40];
char s6[ 40];

main( )
{
        printf("sl initially is %s\n",sl);
        copy_l(s2,sl);
        printf("s2 is now %s\n" ,s2);


        printf("s3 initially is %s\n",s3);
        copy_1 (s3,"C Programming is Totally Tubular");
        printf("s3 now is %s\n",s3);


        printf("s4 initially is %s\n",s4);
        copy_2(s4,sl);
        printf("s4 now is %s\n",s4);


        printf("s5 initially is %s\n",s5);
        copy_2(s5,"C Programming is Totally Tubular");
        printf("s5 now is %s\n" ,s5);


        printf("sl => %s s6 => %s \n",sl,s6);
        strcpy(s6,s 1);
        printf("sl => %s s6 => %s \n",sl,s6);
}
```
sl initially is Terrill Owens
s2 is now Terrill Owens
s3 initially is
s3 now is C Programming is Totally Tubular
s4 initially is
s4 now is Terrill Owens
s5 initially is
s5 now is C Programming is Totally Tubular
s 1 => Terrill Owens s6 =>
s 1 => Terrill Owens s6 => Terrill Owens

Exercise 21

/* write a C function that will determine the length

       of a user input string, use pointers and try to make it

       as efficient as possible */

/* Use the strlen built-in function to check your work */

Solution For Exercise 21

```c
/* edgar.c */
int slength ( char * string ptr )
{
        char * cptr = string_ptr;

        while ( *cptr++ );

        return ( cptr - string_ptr - 1);
}


main( )
{
        int slength ( char * string );
        printf("%i ", slength(" 12345") );
        printf("%i ",  slength(""));
        printf("%i ",slength("12345678901234567890 12345") );
        printf("\n");

}
```

prog73.c   printf in depth

How to print integers

%i	integer base 10
%o	integer base 8
%x	integer base 16
%u	unsigned integer

%x	integer base 16, lower case letters
%X	integer base 16, upper case letters
%#x	integer base 16, lower case letters, leading Ox
%#X	integer base 16, upper case letters, leading OX

```
#define PR printf
main( )
{
        int prec;  float f;  int w;

        PR("Integer Examples:\n");
        PR("\tbase 10 \tbase 8 \tbase 16\tunsigned int \n");
        PR("\t%i\t\t%o\t%x\t%u\n\n", 123, 123, 123, 123);
        PR("\tbase 16\t\tbase16 all caps\tbase16 with leading x\tbase16 with CAPS & X\n");
        PR("\t%x\t\t%X\t\t\t%#X\t\t%#X\n\n",1007,1007,1007,1007);
        PR("\tbase 10, sign\tbase10, lead space, base 10 rjust, fw 7,0 fill");
        PR("\t base 10,7 digits min fw\n");
        PR("\t%+i\t\t% i\t\t\t%07i\t\t\t\t% .7i\n\n", 1 ,2,3,4);


        PR("\nString Examples:\n");

        PR("\tpercent s only, string in field sized to fit\n");
        PR("\t1234567890123456789012345678901234567890\n");
```

244

```
PR("\t%s\n\n","the quick brown fox jumped over the lazy dog");
PR("\tpercent .5s first five chars from string\n");
PR("\t12345678901234567890123456789012345678901234567890\n");
PR("\t%.5s\n\n","the quick brown fox jumped over the lazy dog");
PR("\tpercent 30s at least thirty chars from string\n");
PR("\11234567 8901234567890123456789012345678901234567890\n");
PR("\t%30s\n\n","the quick brown fox jumped over the lazy dog");
PR("\tpercent 20.5 s five chars, rjust in a field 20 wide\n");
PR("\t1234567890 1234567890123456789012345678901234567 890\n");
PR("\t%20.5s\n\n","the quick brown fox jumped over the lazy dog");
PR("\tpercent - 20.5 s five chars, ljust in a field 20 wide\n");
PR("\t1234567890 1234567890 1234567890 1234567890 1234567890\n");
PR("\t%-20.5sf\n\n","the quick brown fox jumped over the lazy dog");
```

```
PR("Float Examples:\n");
PR("\t7 .2f\1\17 .5f\t\t1.5f of 12345.67890\n");
PR("\t \n");
PR("\t% 7 .2f \1%7 .5f\1% 1.5t\n\n", 12345.67890, 12345.67890, 12345.67890);
PR("\t7 .2f\1\17 .5fWl.5f of 1.2345\n");
PR("\t \n");
PR("\t% 7 .2f \1%7 .5f\1% 1.5t\n\n", 1.2345, 1.2345, 1.2345);


/* special cases where the precision is an argument */
PR("Enter a float\n");
scanf("%f' ,&f);
PR("Enter number of digits after decimal to display\n");
scanf("%i",&prec);
PR("\n.................................");
PR("%.*t\n\n", prec,f);


/* special case where the precision and total field width are an argument */
PR("Enter a fioat\n");
scanf("% f' ,&f);
PR("Enter number of digits after decimal to display\n");
scanf("%i" ,&prec);
PR("Enter total field width \n");
scanf("%i",&w);
PR("   \n");
PR("%*. *f\n", w,prec,f);


PR("\nCharacters:\n");
PR(" 123456789012345678901234567890123456789012345678901234567890\n");
PR("%c%3c\n", 'W', 'W');

}
```

INTEGERS

%+i   print the sign character

% i   force a leading space in front of a positive

%07i   right justified, 7 digit width, zero leading fill

%.7i   minimum field with 7 digits, right justified, leading zeroes

FLOATS

%8.2f   total field width eight, two decimal positions

%.*f",x,d)   default field width, x decimal positions

%*.*f',x,y,d) total field width x, y decimal positions

The Strings

%s   null terminated string

%5s   first five characters (or until delimiter)

%.5s   first five characters (forget delimiter)

%20.5s   five characters, right justified in 20 character field

%-20.5s   five characters, left justified in 20 character field

scanf modifiers

%s   read in a string delimited by ws or null

%5s   read in up to 5 characters delimited by ws or null

%5s: %5s$%5s   read in up to 5 characters until : delimiter

                       read in up to 5 characters until $ delimiter

                       read in up to 5 characters

%[abc]s   read in characters until ws, null or non abc encountered

%[^abc]s   read in characters until ws, null or abc encountered

%i %c   read in integer, consume ws, read in charater

% i%c   read in integer, do not consume ws, read in character

prog74.c scanf in depth

```
/* program to illustrate reading using scanf */

/* clearly demonstrates the next scanf picking up */
/* where the last scanf left off */
main ( )
{
        char c;
        char s[60];
        int i;

        i = scanf("%c",&c);
        printf("i = %d c => %e\n",i, c);
        i = scanf("%s",s);
        printf("i = %d s => %s\n",i,s);

        i = scanf("%5s",s);
        printf("i = %d s => %s\n",i,s);

        i = scanf("%[abc]",s);
        printf("i = %d s=> %s\n",i,s);

        i = scanf("%[^abc]",s);
        printf("i = %d s => %s\n",i,s);
}
```

input file:
the alphabet abcdefghijklmnopqrstuvwxyz
the alphabet abcdefghijklmnopqrstuvwxyz
the alphabet abcdefghijklmnopqrstuvwxyz
the alphabet abcdefghijklmnopqrstuvwxyz
the alphabet abcdefghijklmnopqrstuvwxyz
the alphabet abcdefghijklmnopqrstuvwxyz
the alphabet abcdefghijklmnopqrstuvwxyz
the alphabet abcdefghijklmnopqrstuvwxyz

program output
i = 1   c => t
i = 1   s => he
i = 1   s => alpha
i = 1   s => b
i = 1   s => et

prog75.c   scanf in depth

```c
/* attempts to fix scanf idiosyncracies */
main ( )
{
        char c; char trash[80]; char s[80];
        int i; int j;
        char sl[80]; char s2[80]; char s3[80];

        /* read the first character into c */
        /* read the rest of the line into trash */
        i = scanf("%c%[^\n]\n" ,&c,trash);
        printf("i = %d c => %c trash => %s\n",i, c, trash);

        /* clean out both of the buffers */
        for ( i = 0; i < 80; i++ )
        {
                trash[i] = s[i] = 0x00;
        }

        i = scanf("%s%[^\n]\n",s,trash);
        printf("i = %d s => %s trash => %s\n",i,s);

        for ( i = 0; i < 80; i++ )
        {
                trash[i] = s[i] = 0x00;
        }

        i = scanf("%5s%[ ^\n]\n" ,s,trash);
        printf("i = %d s => %s trash => %s\n",i,s);
        for ( i  = 0; i < 80; i++ )
        {
                trash[i] = s[i] = 0x00;
```

```c
}


        i = scanf("%[abc]%[^\n]\n",s,trash);
        printf("i = %d s=> %s trash => %s\n",i,s);


        for ( i = 0; i < 80; i++ )
        {
                trash[i] = s[i] = 0x00;
        }


        i = scanf("%[^abc]%[^\n]\n",s,trash);
        printf("i = %d s => %s trash => %s\n",i,s);


        /* read the line as three white space separated strings */
        i = scanf("%s %s %s",sl,s2,s3);
        printf("sl => %s\n",sl);
        printf("s2 => %s\n",s2);
        printf("s3 => %s\n",s3);
}
```

input file

File Input Pointer

the alphabet abcdefghijk1mnopqrstuvwxyz
the alphabet abcdefghijk1mnopqrstuvwxyz
the alphabet abcdefghijk1mnopqrstuvwxyz
the alphabet abcdefghijk1mnopqrstuvwxyz
the alphabet abcdefghijk1mnopqrstuvwxyz
the alphabet abcdefghijk1mnopqrstuvwxyz
the alphabet abcdefghijk1mnopqrstuvwxyz
the alphabet abcdefghijk1mnopqrstuvwxyz

sample output
i = 2   c => t   trash => he alphabet abcdefghijklmnopqrstuvwxyz
i = 2   s => the   trash => alphabet abcdefghijklmnopqrstuvwxyz
i = 2   s => the   trash => alphabet abcdefghijklmnopqrstuvwxyz
i = 0   s=>   trash =>
i = 2   s => the   trash => alphabet abcdefghijklmnopqrstuvwxyz
sl => the
s2 => alphabet
s3 => abcdefghijklmnopqrstuvwxyz

Sample Run (Illustrates logical operations)

Anding things together

And of

10001111

00000011

00000011

Oring things together

Or of

10001111

00000011

10001111

Xoring things together

Xor of

10001111

00000011

10001100

One's complementing things

One's complement of

10001111

01110000

One's complement of

00000011

11111100

prog67.c   Bit Operations

```
/* and                 &      */
/* inclusive or        |      */
/* exclusive or        ^      */
/* ones complement     ~      */
/* left shift          <<     */
/* right shift         >>     */


disp_binary(c)
char c;
 {
        int i;
        for ( i = 0; i < 8; i++ )
        {
                if (c & 0x80)
                        printf(" 1 ");
                else
                        printf("0");
                c = c << 1;    /* left shift c by one bit */
                               /* the high bit shifted out goes in 'bit bucket' */
        }
        printf("\n");
}
```

```
main ( )
{
        char a,b,result;

        printf(" Anding things together \n");
        printf("And of\n");
        a = Ox8f;        /* 1000 1111 */
        disp_binary(a);
        b = Ox03;        /* 0000 0011 */
        disp_binary(b);
        result = a & b;        /* if either bit is zero, result is 0 */
        disp_binary(result);   /* if both bits are one, result is 1 */
        printf("\n");

        printf("Oring things together \n");
        printf("Or of\n");
        a = Ox8f;        /* 1000 1111 */
        disp_binary(a);
        b = Ox03;        /* 0000 0011 */
        disp_binary(b);
        result = a | b;        /* if either bit is one, result is one */
        disp_binary(result);
        printf("\n");

        printf("Xoring things together \n");
        printf("Xor of\n");
        a = Ox8f;        /* 1000 1111 */
        disp_binary(a);
        b = Ox03;        /* 0000 0011 */
        disp_binary(b);
        result = a ^ b;        /* if only one bit is one, result is one */
        disp_binary(result);
        printf("\n");
```

```c
printf("One's complementing things \n");
printf("One's complement of\n");
a = Ox8f;        /* 1000 1111 */
disp_binary(a);
a = ~a;          /* switch 1 to 0, and 0 to 1 */
disp_binary(a);
printf("\n");

printf("One's complement of\n");
b = Ox03;        /* 0000 0011 */
disp_binary(b);
b = ~b;
disp_binary(b);
printf("\n");
```

Exercise 22

/* write a c program that will accept a number from the user

       display it in hexadecimal format then

       display it in binary format, one bit at a time

       each bit on a separate line */

Solution For Exercise 22

```
/* bits.c */
/* input a positive integer number
        display it in hex
        display it in binary
        display it one bit per line, from high to low
        for added challenge, leave off any leading zeroes
*/
main( )
{
        int i,x,ptr;
        int last one;
        int bits[8 * sizeof(x)];

        printf("Enter number \n");
        scanf("%i",&x);
        printf("%i base 10 0x%x base 16 ",x,x);
        for ( i = 0; i < 8 * sizeof(x); i++ )
        {
                bits[i] = x & (int) 1;
                x = x >> 1;
                if ( bits[i] == 1 )
                        lastone = i;
        }
                while ( last_one >= 0 )
                        printf("%i" ,bits[last_one--]);

        printf(" base 2 \n");
}
```

Enter num ber
5
5 base 10   0x5 base 16   101 base 2

Enter number
127
127 base 10   Ox7f base 16   1111111 base 2

--- -

prog71.c

#ifdef   compiler keyword conditional compilation

```
/* program to illustrate #ifdef */
/* this program will be compiled and run several times */
/* on each compile, I will define BEFORE or AFTER differently *
/* on each compile, I  will define BEFORE or AFTER differently */
main ( )
{
        int i;
        int sum;


        sum = 0;
        for ( i = 0; i < 10; i++ )
        {
#ifdef BEFORE
        printf("before addition sum = %d i = %d \n",sum,i);
#endif
                sum = sum + i;
#ifdef AFTER
        printf("after addition sum = %d i = %d \n",sum,i);
#endif
        }
        printf("sum is %d \n",sum);
}


acc –o prog71 prog71.c
sum is 45


acc -D BEFORE -o prog71 prog71.c
before addition sum = 0 i = 0
before addition sum = 0 i  = 1
before addition sum = 1 i = 2
```

before addition sum = 3 i = 3

before addition sum = 6 i = 4

before addition sum = 10 i = 5

before addition sum = 15 i = 6

before addition sum = 21 i = 7

before addition sum = 28 i = 8

before addition sum = 36 i = 9

sum is 45

acc -D BEFORE -D AFfER -o prog71 prog71.c

before addition sum = 0 i = 0

after addition sum = 0 i = 0

before addition sum = 0 i = 1

after addition sum = 1 i = 1

before addition sum = 1 i = 2

after addition sum = 3 i = 2

before addition sum = 3 i = 3

after addition sum = 6 i = 3

before addition sum = 6 i = 4

after addition sum = 10 i = 4

before addition sum = 10 i = 5

after addition sum = 15 i = 5

before addition sum = 15 i = 6

after addition sum = 21 i = 6

before addition sum = 21 i = 7

after addition sum = 28 i = 7

before addition sum = 28 i = 8

after addition sum = 36 i = 8

before addition sum = 36 i = 9

after addition sum = 45 i = 9

sum is 45

acc -D Before -D After -o prog71 prog71.c

sum is 45

Appendix: Warning about order of evaluation

It is important (critical) to note that:

"the order of evaluation of subexpressions in a C expression where the order of evaluation is not

defined is not defined".

This means that the statement:

a = b + c;

only implies that b and c are added and the result stored in a.

We can make no guarantee which will be retrieved first , a or b.

If we have 2 functions that return integers fl and f2:

int c;

c = fl( ) + f2( );

we cannot state which function, fl or f2, will be executed

first.

likewise:

int c = 7;

int a;

a = c + c++;

a will have either the value 14 (7 + 7) or 15 (8+7).

We cannot state which it will be and be sure that the answer will be the same on all

systems.

int i = 9;

printf("%i %i", i, ++i);

will print either 9 10

or   10 10

this usually does not present any problems, but the programmer should be aware

of it.

RECCOMMENDATION: NEVER make a second reference to a variable being modified

in the same expression where the order of evaluation is undefined. Dennis Ritchie used to

say that "such and such is undefined"   What he meant was, "if you try to do the undefined

thing then the results will most likely be something other than what you expected". Then

he would smile and say "Garbage In, Garbage Out", or sometimes just "GIGO"

quicksort.c   a quicksort example

```c
#include <stdio.h>
#include <math.h>
#define        MAXQUICK        128
int quick[MAXQUICK]        /* array that holds the data */
int quickindex;          /* index of how many elements there are */
FILE * fd; FILE * fd 1;


main ( )
{
        void printdata(void);
        void sortdata(int start pos, int end_pos);
        int intemp; int c;
        fd = fopen("datafile","r");
        if ( fd == NULL )
         {
                printf("open 1 failed \n");
                exit( -1);
         }


        fd1 = fopen("quickout" ,"w");
        if (fd1 == NULL )
         {
                printf("open2 failed \n");
                exit( -2);
         }


        /* input the data from file */
        quickindex = 0;
        while ( fscanf(fd, " %d", &intemp) != EOF)
         {
                /* store data in array */
```

```c
                quick[quickindex++] = intemp;
        }
        quickindex--;

        /* print original list of data */
        printf("ORIGINAL LIST\n");
        printdata( );
        printf("\n\n");
        sortdata(0,quickindex);

        printdata( );
        close(fd); close(fdl);
}

void
printdata(void)
{
        int i;
        fprintf(fd 1 ,"\n\n");
        for ( i = 0; i <= quickindex; i++ )
        {
                printf(" %d ",quick[i]);
                fprintf(fd 1, " %d ",quick[i]);
        }
        printf("\n\n");
        fprintf(fd1,"/n");
        return;
} /* end printdata * /
```

```c
#define        UP      0
#define        DOWN           1

void sortdata(int start_pos, int end_pos)
{
        int temp;
        int target_pos;
        int direction = DOWN;
        int in_end_pos;
        int in_start_pos;
        int temp_lower, temp_upper;

        in_start_pos = start_pos;
        in_end_pos = end_pos;
        target_pos = start_pos;

        temp_lower = start_pos;
        temp_upper = end_pos;

        printf("SORTDATA %i %i \n",start_pos,end_pos);
        printdata( );
        fprintf(fdl,"SORTDATA %i %i \n",start_pos,end_pos);

    if ( start_pos >= end_pos )
            return;
    while (temp_lower < temp_upper)
    {
            if (direction == DOWN)
            {
                    if (quick[temp_upper] >= quick[target_pos] )
                    {
                            /* no update, move pointer */
                            temp_upper--;
```

```
              }
          else
          {
                  /* swap values */
                  temp = quick[temp_upper];
                  quick[temp_upper] = quick[target_pos];
                  quick[target_pos] = temp;
                  printdata( );

                  /* change direction of travel */
                  direction = UP;
                  /* change pointer to target value */
                  target_pos = temp_upper;
          }
      }
  else /* direction of travel is UP */
  {
          if ( quick[temp_lower] <= quick[target_pos])
                  temp _lower++;
          else
          {
                  /* swap values */
                  temp = quick[temp_lower];
                  quick[temp_lower] = quick[target_pos];
                  quick[target_pos] = temp;
                  printdata( );
                  /* change direction of travel */
                  direction = DOWN;
                  /* change pointer to target value */
                  target_pos = temp_lower;
          }
      }
} /* end while */
```

```
/* at this point the left and right pointers have met or crossed */
/* now we have divided our list into two segments */
        /* sort each of the smaller segments */


        /* RECURSION */
        /* do left side */
        if ( in_start_pos < target_pos - 1 )
        {
                printf("Calling left side \n");
                sortdata(in_start_pos, target_pos - 1);
        }


        /* do the right side */
        if ( target_pos + 1 < in_end_pos )
        {
                printf("Calling right side \n");
                sortdata(targetpos + 1 ,in_end_pos);
        }
        return;
} /* end sortdata */
```

ptrtofunc.c   Pointers To Functions

```c
void exit( );

static void proca(fno,al,a2,a3,a4,aS)
int fno,al,a2,a3,a4,aS;
{
        int stat;
        stat = printf("In proca\n");
        if ( stat == 0 )
                exit(stat);


        stat = printf("%i %i %i %i %i %i\n",fno,al,a2,a3,a4,aS);
        if ( stat == 0 )
                exit(stat);
}


static void procb(fno,al,a2,a3,a4,aS)
int fno,al,a2,a3,a4,aS;
{
        int stat;
        stat = printf("In procb\n");
        if ( stat == 0 )
                exit(stat);
        stat = printf("%x %x %x %x %x %x\n",fno,al,a2,a3,a4,a5);
        if ( stat == 0 )
                exit(stat);
}
```

```c
static void procc(fno,al,a2,a3,a4,a5)
int fno,al,a2,a3,a4,a5;
{
        int stat;
        stat = printf("In procc\n");
        if ( stat == 0 )
                exit(stat);
        stat = printf("%5i %5i %5i %5i %5i %5i\n",fno,al,a2,a3,a4,a5);
        if ( stat == 0 )
                exit(stat);
}


static void ( *procedure_table[ ]) ( )
=
{
        proca,
        procb,
        procc
};


int main ( )
{
        int funcno, arg1, arg2, arg3, arg4, arg5;
        int i,stat;
        funcno = 0;
        argl = 100;
        arg2 = 200;
        arg3 = 300;
        arg4 = 400;
        arg5 = 500;

        stat = printf("In main routine \n");
        if ( stat == 0 )
```

```c
                exit(stat);

        while ( funcno != -1 )
        {
                stat = printf(,'\nEnter function you wish to call\n");
                if ( stat == 0 )
                        exit(stat);
                stat = printf("-1\tquit\nO\tproca\n1\tprocb\n2\tprocc\n");
                if ( stat == 0 )
                        exit(stat);
                stat = scanf("%i",&funcno);
                if ( stat == 0 )
                        exit(stat);
                if (funcno != -1 && funcno >= 0 && funcno <= 2)
                {
                        (*procedure_table[funcno]) ( funcno,argl,arg2,arg3,arg4,arg5);
                }
        } /* end while */
        return(0);
} /* end main */
```

Appendix: Reading complex declarations:

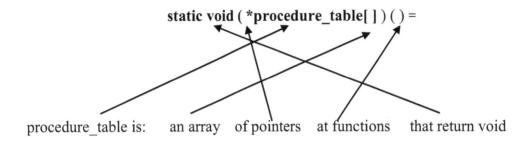

static void (*procedure_table[ ]) ( ) =

procedure_table is: an array   of pointers   at functions   that return void

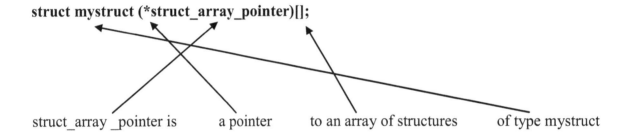

struct mystruct *struct_pointer_array[];

struct_pointer_array is   an array   of pointers   to structures of type mystruct

struct mystruct (*struct_array_pointer)[];

struct_array _pointer is   a pointer   to an array of structures   of type mystruct

Appendix To Brace or Not To Brace

```c
main ( )
{
        int x;
        printf("Enter x \n");
        scanf("%i",&x);
        /* this decision structure is fully braced and indented in the KK style */
        if( x < 10)
        {
                printf("x less than ten \n");
        }
        else if ( x > 10 )
        {
                printf("x is greater than ten \n");
                if ( x < 100 )
                {
                        printf("x less than one hundred\n");
                }
                else
                {
                        printf("x is greater than or equal to 100\n");
                }
        }
        else
        {
                printf("x is exactly ten \n");
        }

        /* this decision structure is not braced, indented only in KK style */
        if ( x < 10 )
                printf("x less than ten \n");
        else if ( x > 10 )
                if ( x < 100 )
                        printf("x less than one hundred\n");
```

```c
        else
                printf("x is greater than or equal to lCXJ\n");
        else
                printf("x is exactly ten \n");


/* this decision structure removes the else from the nested if
        and introduces problem encountered when you leave off the braces */
/* the last else belongs to the if ( x < 100 ) NOT the if (x < 10) */
/* this could have been avoided by bracing */
if ( x < 10)
        printf("x less than ten \n");
else if ( x > 10 )
        if ( x < 100)
                printf("x less than one hundred\n");
else
    printf("x is exactly ten \n");


/* this expression is indented and braced in a K&R like method */
/* decide for yourself which style is most readable and MAINTAINABLE */
if( x < 10){
        printf("x less than ten \n"); }
        else if ( x > 10 ) {
                if (x < 100) {
                        printf("x less than one hundred\n"); }
                        else {
                                printf("x is greater than or equal to 100\n"); } }
                                else { printf("x is exactly ten \n"); }

}
```

Enter x   5

x less than ten

x less than ten

x less than ten

x less than ten

Enter x   11

x is greater than ten

x less than one hundred

x less than one hundred

x less than one hundred

x less than one hundred

Enter x   102

x is greater than ten

x is greater than or equal to 100

x is greater than or equal to 100

x is exactl y ten

x is greater than or equal to 100

NOTES:

Braces with only one statement within them are 'free' (no code overhead).
Experience has taught that there are times when a single statement within a loop or decision structure needs to have a debug statement added. This means that you have to add the braces anyway. Puting them in as an afterthought may lead to problems:

```
if ( value == 9 )          ◄──────────── original code
    call function( );


if ( value == 9 )
    printf("if case true calling function");
    call_function( );  ◄─────── code with debug statement and added bug
                                code should look like this


if ( value == 9)
{
    call function( );
}


if ( value ==9 )  ◄─────── original code
{
    printf("if case true calling function");
    call_function( );
}
```

Appendix

```c
main ( )
{
        int i,j;
        int x[5] = { 1 , 2 , 3, 4, 5 };
        int y[2][3] = { {10,20,30}, {100, 200, 300} };
        printf("AAA \n");
        for ( i =0; i  < 5; i++ )
                /* this works as you'd expect */
                printf("%i ",x[i]);


        printf("\n\n");
        printf("BBB\n");
        for ( i= 0; i < 5; i++ )
                /* THIS ALSO WORKS !!! */
        /* compiler knows i is of type int and x is of type pointer to int
                and it generates the address correctly */
                printf("%i ",i[x]);


        printf("\n\n");
        printf("CCC\n");
        for ( i = 0; i < 2; i++ )
        {
                for ( j = 0; j < 3; j++ )
                {
                        /* this works as you'd expect */
                        printf("%i ",y[i][j]);
                }
                printf("\n");
        }
```

```
                printf("\n\n");
                printf("DDD\n");
                for ( i = 0; i < 2; i++ )
                {
                        for ( j = 0; j < 3; j++ )
                        {
                                /* THIS ALSO WORKS !!! */
                                /* compiler knows y is of type pointer to pointer to int
                                        and i and j are of type int, figures out address correctly */
                                printf("%i ",i[y][j]):
                        }
                        printf("\n");
                }

printf("\n\n");
#if 0
        /* this would be a compiler error */
        printf("EEE\n");
        for ( i = 0; i < 2; i++ )
        {
                for (j = 0; j < 3; j++ )
                {
                        /* THIS would not work, compiler error I DON'T KNOW WHY */
                        printf("%i ",i[j] [y]);
                }
                printf("\n");
        }
#endif
}

AAA
12345

BBB
12345

CCC
10 20 30
100 200 300

DDD
10 20 30
100 200 300
```

Crazy Address Stuff

```
int i;

int array[5];

for(i=0; i<5; i++ )
    printf("%i \n",
    array[i]);


for(i=0; i<5; i++ )
    printf("%i \n",
    i[array]);
```

Both these loops do the same thing: print out the contents of the array.

This is because array[i] is compiled as *(array+i) which is the same as *(i+array).

With a 2 dimensional array, the first index (major index) is itself an adderss, so in our example:

```
int i,j;
int y[2][3] = { {10,20,30}, {1
00,200,300} };
for ( i = 0; i < 2; i++ )
        for ( j = 0; j < 3; j++)
                printf("%i ",y[i][j]);
```

y[i][j] means *(*(y+i) +j) where i is the offset into the array of row addresses

and j is the offset into that row

```
for ( i = 0; i < 2; i++ )
        for ( j = 0; j < 3; j++ )
                printf("%i ",i[y][j]);
```

i[y][j] means *(*(i+y)+j) which also works since it generates the same address as in the

previous example


```
for ( i = 0; i < 2; i++ )
        for ( j = 0; j < 3; j++ )
                printf("%i ",i[j][y]);
```

i[j][y] means *(*(i+j) +y) which results in a compiler error since we are attempting to
add 2 integers (i and j) and then dereference them.

APPENDIX

Some terminals don't have keys for (haracters that you may need in a C program.

The C language can handle this to a certain extent.

The mechanism employed to deal with this situation is the trigraph.

The following three keystrokes, when used together with no spaces between them, refer to the indicated character on their right.

This technique is useful in the 3270 enviroment because the [and] characters are not found on the 3270 keyboard.

sequence

??=	#
??(	[
??)	]
??<	{
??>	}
??/	\
??'	^
??!	|
??-	~

After JT Decided He Couldn't Write One More Program....

He Started Writing Novels,

Please Consider Reading The Pattern (it's about a programming error)

Or Consider Sampling Others of JT Kalnay's Novels

 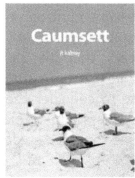 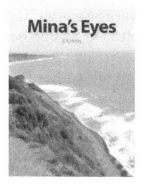

The first of JT Kalnay's works I've read, this early effort compares nicely with Ryan's "Adolescence of P-1" or Grisham's "The Firm" but wisely navigates around Powers' "Galatea 2.2" territory. You get a good sense this writer has "been there" but there is more to "The Pattern" than just an insider's view of an industry and culture that is pretty much a black box to those that haven't. This one gets a 4 out of 5 simply for not quite cracking the level of the big boys: Clancy, Ludlum, Cussler et al. Will be interested to see how this author develops in this genre.

I was surprised to enjoy this book so much as it comes from a not so well known author. Fantastic fiction.

I was thinking about the HAL 9000 malfunction in 2001 A Space Odyssey while reading The Pattern. Decades ago, I wondered if people would risk their lives on software. Now we have fly-by-wire controls in our airplanes and we depend on software in our hospital equipment as well as our cars. Software glitches can now kill. It's a really scary thought and I really enjoyed the thrilling journey the author takes us on in this techno-thriller treat. In the best spirit of science fiction it gives us pause to consider the dependency we freely give to our technology. In addition, as this story unfolds our humanity is laid bare in the face of technological realities that are seldom realized by most of us.

Please Enjoy This Sample From The Pattern

June 19, 1994

Chantilly Virginia

Assembled From News Wire Reports

A chartered executive Lear Jet inbound from Mexico City crashed today in heavy fog during final approach to Dulles National Airport in Washington D.C. Ten passengers and two crew members were killed instantly. There were no Americans on the flight and there were no survivors. Although the airplane had the latest electronics, it had aborted one landing due to the fog and was in the process of lining up for a second attempt when the accident occurred. The black box flight recorder has been recovered from the wreckage and the bodies have been identified. The last transmission from the cockpit was, "There seems to be something wrong with the electronics. Going around." The plane disappeared from radar less than ten seconds later.

June 20, 1994

San Francisco, California

Thin clouds drifted high above the city by the Bay. Craig and Stacey sat behind the APSoft building on the large cedar deck. A gentle breeze caressed Stacey's long, summer golden hair. Craig was having a very hard time concentrating on the report in his hands.

"Do you want to hear something weird?" Stacey asked.

"I don't know. Do I?" Craig answered.

"Yes. You do," Stacey said.

"Okay. Let's have it," Craig said.

"We're three for three this year," Stacey said.

"I don't get it," Craig said.

"On airplane crashes. We're three for three."

"I still don't get it," Craig said.

"Listen. First you know that guy in Turkey where the Blackhawks got shot down. Second, we both know Rakesh who's been in Hong Kong where the plane that crashed in Nagoya originated. Third, my friend in Mexico works for that company that chartered that plane that crashed in Virginia the other day. We're three for three."

"Better call the National Enquirer," Craig said.

"Jerk," Stacey said.

"We know somebody at almost every airline or aircraft manufacturer in the world Stacey. It'd be a miracle if we didn't know someone somehow related to every crash," Craig said.

"You're still a jerk," Stacey said.

"Yeah I know. It's part of my charm," he replied.

Stacey made a face at him and rolled her eyes.

"Please," she said.

"But you know what? You've piqued my curiosity. I'm going to do some research and see how many wrecks there have been in the last year. It does seem like there's been an unusual amount doesn't it?" Craig asked.

"Nice try," Stacey said.

"No. I'm totally serious. Now that you've pointed it out, I really am curious."
"Um huh," she said dismissively.

"Ready to throw it some more," Stacey asked, dangling Craig's birthday Frisbee on the end of a long slender finger.

"Not right now," Craig said. I better get started on that research.

JT Kalnay is an attorney and an author. He has been an athlete, a soldier, a professor, a programmer, an Ironman, and mountain climber. JT now divides his time between being an attorney, being an author, and helping his wife chase after seven nieces and nephews.

JT was born and raised in Belleville, Ontario, Canada. Growing up literally steps from the Bay of Quinte, water, ice, fishing, swimming, boating, and drowning were very early influences and appear frequently in his work.

Educated at the Royal Military College, the University of Ottawa, the University of Dayton, and Case Western Reserve University, JT has spent countless hours studying a wide range of subjects including math, English, computer science, physics, and law. Many of his stories are set on college campuses. JT (along with MC and KR) is one of the founding members of the Stone Frigate Military Academy English Society.

JT is a certified rock climbing guide and can often be found atop crags in West Virginia, California, Texas, New Mexico, Nevada, Kentucky, Mexico, and Italy. Rock climbing appears frequently in his writing.

JT has witnessed firsthand many traumatic events including the World Trade Center Bombing, the Long Island Railroad Shooting, a bear attack, a plane crash, and numerous fatalities, in the mountains and elsewhere.

Disasters, loss, and confronting personal fear are common themes in his writing.

www.jtkalnay.com